KU-756-486

THE LESLIE PRICE MEMORIAL LIBRARY

FIELD HOUSE

BRADFIELD COLLEGE

FROM EARLY LIFE

Works by the same author

NOVELS (*as H.S. Hoff*):

Three Girls: a trilogy:
  Trina
  Rhéa
  Lisa
Three Marriages

  (*as William Cooper*):
Scenes from Life: a trilogy:
  Scenes From Provincial Life (with an introduction by Malcolm
    Bradbury)
  Scenes From Metropolitan Life
  Scenes From Married Life
Scenes From Later Life (a companion volume to the trilogy)
The Struggles Of Albert Woods
The Ever-Interesting Topic
Disquiet And Peace
Young People
Memoirs Of A New Man
You Want The Right Frame of Reference
Love On The Coast
You're Not Alone

PLAY
Prince Genji (adapted from *The Tale of Genji* by Lady Murasaki)

DOCUMENTARY
Shall We Ever Know? (an account of the trial of the Hosein
  brothers for the murder of Mrs McKay)

PAMPHLET
C. P. Snow (British Council Series: *Writers and their work*:
  No. 113)

FROM
EARLY LIFE

William Cooper

MACMILLAN
LONDON

Copyright © William Cooper 1990

All rights reserved. No reproduction, copy or transmission
of this publication may be made without written permission.
No paragraph of this publication may be reproduced, copied
or transmitted save with written permission or in
accordance with the provisions of the Copyright Act 1956
(as amended). Any person who does any unauthorised act
in relation to this publication may be liable to criminal
prosecution and civil claims for damages.

First published 1990 by
MACMILLAN LONDON LIMITED
4 Little Essex Street London WC2R 3LF
and Basingstoke

Associated companies in Auckland, Delhi, Dublin, Gaborone,
Hamburg, Harare, Hong Kong, Johannesburg, Kuala Lumpur,
Lagos, Manzini, Melbourne, Mexico City, Nairobi, New York,
Singapore and Tokyo

A CIP catalogue record for this book is available from the
British Library.

ISBN 0-333-52367-9

Typeset by Macmillan Production Ltd

Printed in Great Britain by Billings and Sons Ltd, Worcester

I

I've always said I can't write an autobiography, for the simple reason that I can't remember what happened. When I was young my memory was below par; now I'm old it's beyond hope. Being persuaded to try and write something, I can't do more than dredge up random bits of debris from my past, since I have no diary and no letters, plus an aesthetic objection to 'research' – the nature of remembering is poetic.

II

'I remember, I remember . . . '

Precious little, now it comes to the crunch – and *that* not specially accurate, either.

I don't remember being born. That happened, I'm told, on the 4th of August 1910. On the whole I don't regret it; nor do I bear it against my parents, intelligent and decent-minded schoolteachers both, who unfailingly did their best for me. I had a happy childhood, I think. My real name is Harry Hoff, and I clearly remember days when my schoolfellows called me Happy Hoff.

III

Astonishingly to me I can dredge up recollections from my perambulator, or rather pushchair days, when I must have been aged two. The first has stayed as sharp and vivid as it was the day it happened. I was being wheeled down a street with a high brick wall on one side and a roadway on the other, the road being crossed further down by a railway-bridge. (As the town was Crewe – then as now a notable railway-junction – it's not surprising that there were plenty of railway-bridges around.) We stopped suddenly. 'Look, Harry!' I looked. In the stretch of grey sky above the bridge a black object was buzzing towards us.

'That's an *aeroplane!*' I went on looking. 'Do you see the aeroplane?'

I saw it and have never forgotten it. (The year was 1912, I suppose, and this must have been one of the first aeroplanes ever seen flying over the town. The name of Harry Hawker floats through my memory – can that be so?)

We watched it going overhead. Then – 'Look at *that!*'

'That' was a blob of liquid on the oilcloth apron covering my legs. 'It's from the aeroplane!' I more or less understood. A drop of liquid from that buzzing object in the sky had fallen on me. A souvenir! No wonder I have always remembered it, incredible and implausible though it seems.

Of course one of the troubles with memory is that given long enough it ceases to distinguish between what actually happened and what one has been told happened. My faith in the incident's having actually happened was partially shaken later when I was sitting in a university physics lecture on surface tension – surely a large drop of oil falling from that height would have broken into small droplets by the time it reached the ground?

Yet I can still, I repeat still, see that black buzzing machine in the stretch of grey sky above the bridge, and the blob of iridescent liquid lying on the shiny black oilcloth over my legs. I remember.

IV

My second recollection from the pushchair days is trifling and common: it is of falling out of the said pushchair. It happened in the backyard of my maternal step-grandmother's house. The yard was paved with bricks of a bluish colour. I had been left on my own, and had managed to worm my way round in the harness which held me – so as to be able to stand and face backwards. I leaned against the handle and the pushchair tipped up. My exact recollection is not of the pain of hitting my head on the ground, nor of the commotion of people rushing out to rescue me; but of the *colour* of the bricks as they came up to hit me. Unforgettably a glistening slatey-blue . . .

V

And another trifling accident sometime in these earliest days. I was sitting in a child's chair, not a 'high' chair but a low one slightly below table level; it had a D-shaped tray which was swung over the back of the chair while one was being installed in it, and then swung forward over one's head so as to keep one safely trapped. There were two people sitting up at the table on either side of me, and one passed a cup and saucer to the other above me head. The cup fell sideways, and the liquid in it spilt over me. What I most clearly remember – and I do remember – is the rattle of the cup in the saucer and the deluge of warm liquid on my hair.

From that day on I refused to drink tea. It was not until I got up to the university that I had to drink it, because it sounded too silly, when I was invited out to tea in his rooms by some fellow undergraduate, to say, 'Do you happen to have a glass of milk?' Yet to this day I dislike lukewarm tea – the *smell* of it nauseates me.

VI

This reminds me that milk was the staple drink of my childhood. My parents always did their best for me, and my mother saw to it that I had good sustaining food, milk standing high on the list for building and sustaining the body. I always drank it cold. Those were the days before everyone, from the highest to all but the very lowest, had a refrigerator. Things were kept cold in our pantry, where the main feature was a large thick shelf made of marble, known as 'the slab'. I can remember the milkman at the door, ladling out our daily order from a large can into one or more jugs which we carried into the pantry and deposited on the slab. Each jug was then covered over with a circle of muslin, whose edge was weighted down by a row of beautiful opaque glass beads, milky sky-blue, leaf-green, buttery yellow . . . So beautiful they would have encouraged anyone to drink milk as first choice, even if his experience of tea had *not* been having it spilt over his head.

VII

Thus was one bit of my behaviour fixed from the age of two: I refused to drink tea till I was nearly twenty. (Makes you think, doesn't it? Of that grisly Jesuit maxim – 'Give us a child till it's seven, etc.')

VIII

A last recollection from the pushchair days, this time of a different order – my first encounter with the Anglican Church, in the shape of a clergyman with red hair. I can't possibly be remembering this merely because I've been told about it.

To introduce a touch of plausibility necessitates my coming out with a revelation which can't help but make me seem immodest about my physical appearance. My parents told me that on holiday they once entered me in a competition for The Most Beautiful Baby in Blackpool, and I won it. (That's as may be: in the matter of looks I can only say my career ever since then has been downhill all the way.) It is not entirely out of the question, in that case, that a well-disposed clergyman, vicar of a church close to the school where my father taught, should stop us in the street and admire the child in the pushchair. He was portly, with small hands and feet – I can still see him, recreate his appearance whole – with spectacles and short red hair, so red as to have an almost greenish tinge. He leaned over the pushchair, smiling at me. 'Hello, little man!' I was terrified.

The incident recurred on the same road leading down to the school, and I was terrified every time. When I started walking to the school I was terrified of going by myself, and was always trying to get someone to accompany me. I had taken it into my head that he wanted to steal me from my parents, and somehow I was unable to tell them. (I can see now that I felt the same sensation of being unable to speak that one experiences in a nightmare.)

My terror lasted long enough to overlap my lighting upon the word 'abduct'. (At the age of six I loved picking up classy words. At seventy-six and more I love chucking them out – Make Things Simple! is my rule now.) As I have never employed an analyst I have no explanation. Fortunately it was what we writers call a 'one-off experience': if I'd found I was terrified of being abducted by every red-haired clergyman I have ever met since, I should of course have employed an analyst.

IX

'*I remember, I remember* . . . ' I can't remember '*the house where I was born*', perhaps not surprisingly, as we left it a few months later.

But I can remember well, astonishingly well, the house we moved to, where we lived until I was eleven. It seemed to me then pretty large. (I suppose if I went back to it now

– I may say I haven't the slightest intention of doing so –
if I went back now, being several times larger myself, it
would seem to me several times smaller.) It was double-
fronted, the larger of the two rooms at the front, the 'big
sitting-room', having a bay-window set back only a few feet
from the pavement – a splendid vantage-point for observing
passers-by. Of the other rooms there were enough comfort-
ably to accommodate throughout the War my father's sister
and her son, a little boy practically the same age as myself.
The Great War broke out on my fourth birthday. A few
months later my father volunteered, was commissioned in
the Royal Garrison Artillery and posted to Flanders for the
duration. Meanwhile the husband of his sister was posted
to West Africa, so she and my cousin Ernie came to live
with us.

For the next four years we two little boys were brought up
together – we were given our meals together, taken to school
together, sent out to play together, sent up to bed together,
or at least sent up to bed at the same time. I have a picture
of our being tucked up in the same bed, but I'm uncertain
of it, because of a recollection from that time – true, when
Ernie was not there – and I was being made to sleep in my
mother's bed. It was Christmas, so perhaps Ernie and his
mother had gone to stay with his father's parents.

I woke in the middle of the night. There was the
mountain of my mother's body under the sheets beside me,
and just beyond the foot of the bed, where my Christmas
stocking was hanging on the brass rail, was standing Father
Christmas in person. I could see him perfectly in the glow
of the night-light, perfectly recognisable by the snowy beard
and the snowy fur trimming round the edge of his hood and
his coat; only the material of his hood and coat, instead
of being bright red, was pure *white*! Now I couldn't have

invented that, though I was unable to convince my mother in the morning. But Ernie, when I told him, believed me.

Those days of our companionship engendered an extraordinary mutual feeling, an extraordinary, almost ludicrous devotion to each other. We resisted being kept apart – perhaps that's why I have the picture of our mothers tucking us up in the same bed together. Our mutual sympathy was such that when something made one of us cry the other began to cry as well. Though I have been told this often, I really can remember its actually happening at least once. We were being pushed along side by side in our pushchairs. (My memory seems to be obsessively focused on pushchairs.) I don't recall why either of us was crying or what caused which of us to begin; but crying we were, in unison. Memorable because being pushed side by side in our pushchairs was more likely to be an occasion for laughing in unison. The axles of his pushchair were misaligned, with the consequence that it kept either running into the side of my pushchair or running off the edge of the pavement: the amusement it caused us was heightened by the exasperation it caused our mothers.

A David and Jonathan, people said. As it were each other's *alter ego* . . . In the light of that, it seems strange to me that I can remember so few specific incidents. I can call up a physical image of him – growing taller and more gangling than me, with a higher forehead and longer face than mine, both of his ears sticking out while only one of mine did; and a small anatomical difference, noticed when we were in the bath together, later to be the subject of boyish comparison and speculation. I suppose that when one is remembering a relationship so harmonious, one's memory tends to dim out the occasions of disharmony. When Ernie and I played together in the garden, we must have competed with each other; but I don't remember any serious trouble or fights breaking out. The only trouble I recall arising from our competing with each other was trouble from our mothers when we were caught standing side by side in the backyard seeing who could wee highest up the coal-house wall.

We were hauled away by the scruff of the neck and sent upstairs for an hour's meditation upon our misdeed. The punishment might conceivably have been more severe had we chosen the wall of the wash-house for our contest The wash-house, in a mode of builder's planning which nowadays might not get local authority approval – unless the said builder happened to be in friendly financial contact with a member of the said authority – adjoined the coal-house. Not that the coal-house was kept anything but as sweet and clean as might be, well stocked in an orderly fashion. It had to be well stocked because the only heating in the house was by coal-fires. Supplies of coal were delivered regularly from a coal-merchant's cart which drew up in the road outside.

Our house was semi-detached: to one side of it there was a narrow passageway, known as 'the entry', down which the coal-merchant's man or men carried the bags of coal, while he remained sitting in his cart, pacifying his horse – apart from occasionally popping into the kitchen for a quick cup of tea. The lumps of coal came in two sizes, the smaller called 'nuts', the larger called 'cobbles'. We bought them by the bag, which held a hundredweight. The bag itself was made of some heavy fibrous material, and had a loop in the middle of each side on the top: the coalman carried it on his shoulders, by catching hold of the two loops at the back of his neck. When he reached the coal-house he let go the outer loop, leaned sharply forward, and dramatically launched an avalanche of coal over the top of his head into a handsome pile in front of him – a spectacle much enjoyed by us two little boys. The lumps of coal had been washed. Shiny and black and crystalline: from them arose the most memorable of attractive tarry smells, recognisable anywhere.

My recollections of the coal-merchant do not end there; but to complete them I shall have to jump ahead by a few years, when a scandal broke out – he absconded with a married woman to whom he regularly delivered his coal. I was old enough to sense moral disapproval in the atmosphere. Yet I overhead what were clearly *jokes* about it – there was one about the milkman regularly delivering his milk to a housewife . . . Now what could that have had to do with it? I wondered.

X

A David and Jonathan; a devotion to each other verging on the ludicrous . . . It depended on our being together, and when we couldn't be together it began to loosen, was bound to loosen. When the War ended Ernie's father returned from West Africa and they went to live in a small town on the Wirral, across the Mersey from the Port of Liverpool. We were separated, and though we continued for ten or more years to stay with each other during school holidays, things were never the same again, and ultimately they faded out. Nevertheless the recollection of our mutual feeling tended to linger in my memory as of an ideal companionship. Looking back on it now, though, I see that I gradually came to recognise it as pretty unrealistic to hold it as an ideal; and when I come to write about times ahead I shall have to confess that I gave it up. Anyway it seems probable to me now, in adulthood, that it could only arise between children of the age Ernie and I were then.

We started school at the beginning of the school-year in 1914, early September, at my father's school, called then a public elementary school, for children between the ages of four and fourteen. The school was divided in two, the 'infants' school' for little boys and girls together, and the two 'big schools' for big boys and big girls separately. Having been taught to read at home I was spared the indignity of the 'babies' class' and, I think, the next class above it. (In those days there were no arguments about children with all degrees of ability being kept together in the same class: it was usual for a bright child to be singled out for early transfer to the class above, for being 'moved up' part-way through the year instead of having to wait till the end of it.) Anyway, it is from that next class that my two most exciting recollections spring up.

One recollection is of my first recognising, first discovering, the English language as such, in the form of lighting upon the pluperfect tense of the verb. I put up my hand –

'Please, Miss Jones, can you say "I *had had*"?' The repetition seemed wonderful to me.

'Of course you can, you clever boy!'

As yet insensitive to irony I preened myself.

The other recollection is of the teacher, while standing by my little desk to look at my work, being called out of the room; and leaving behind, on the desk, the instrument she used for commanding the class's attention. It was like a large peg, made of varnished pale-coloured wood, with a lever set into the side halfway down: when the lever was sharply squeezed against the body, it emitted a loud click. 'Attention, children! . . . ' *Click!* The instrument lay

11

in front of me. (We children sat in pairs at the little desks.) The temptation was irresistible. I picked the instrument up. *Click!* Giggles of applause from the other children. *Click! Click!* . . . Lost to everything in appreciation of my own daring, I didn't notice that the teacher had come back. *Click! Click!* . . .

'Harry Hoff, you naughty boy, what are you doing?'

An unnecessary question. I dropped the clicker too late; and was banished to the corner of the room, there to stand with my face to the wall.

The trouble about being banished to isolation for one's crimes is that mingled with the misery and shame of isolation an element of mischievous pride begins to assert itself. Standing in the corner with my face to the wall, I was singled out from all the other children for being more daring than they were.

In those days being made to stand in the corner of the classroom was a punishment intermediate between being sent, as a last resort, out of the room altogether, and being, for a lesser offence, allowed to stay at one's desk but made to stand up on the seat. Misery-making isolation again, I suppose. I don't remember ever being made to stand up on the seat, myself: what I do remember is the sight of a roomful of cowed children bent over their desks, interspersed with two or three offenders ridiculously standing up high in their midst like statues on pedestals.

Such were the punishments of the individual. There was a different punishment for an obstreperous class as a whole. We were all made to sit motionless with our hands on top of our heads.

XI

On the far side of a large central classroom, the sort of school hall, opposite to where my little classroom was, there were two classrooms marked off by folding partitions made of wooden doors with glass panes at the top. In one of those classrooms taught a friend of my mother's, a friend from their pupil-teacher days: she came to see us at home and I called her Auntie Mag. She comes into the story later on, but I introduce her here because I remember her from then as expert with the loudest, most commanding clicker in the school – one could hear it through the partition and across the hall. She was tall and dark-haired, and she had a soft contralto voice which she never needed to raise in the classroom – she could produce a *Click!* so peremptory that when I was in her class, even I, who knew her familiarly as Auntie Mag, was reduced to instant silence. I don't suppose clickers are used in school any more – they probably wouldn't be heard.

XII

From those early days a recollection of a passing fad enjoyed by Ernie and me – for transfers (known in baby-language as 'stanfers'). A 'stanfer' consisted of a brightly-coloured picture, about four times the size of a postage stamp, printed in what I imagine was a film of gelatine with a paper backing. One soaked the 'stanfer' in a saucer of water, then applied it face downwards to the page of an album, pressed it lightly, and then very carefully tore away the paper backing, leaving the picture transferred. It had to be torn away very carefully indeed or the film carrying the picture was distorted and the result was spoilt. An innocent pastime.

A slightly less innocent variation was to apply the 'stanfer' to a part of one's body – most conveniently to the back of one's hand – when the picture transferred looked like a tattoo. Our mothers were not enthusiastic about this variation, especially as the tattoo was not as easy as all that to scrub off in the bath. The most exciting thing to do, then, was to go to school 'tatooed'.

XIII

So much for my days in the 'infants' school'. My father was a teacher of boys in the 'big school', or rather had been a teacher till he joined the Army. From time to time he came home on leave from Flanders. Passchendaele, Ypres, the Marne, the Somme . . . names impressed on my memory in the first place merely as names overheard, later as standing for battles – and finally as standing for appalling and useless slaughter. I can recall the excitement in the air when my father arrived on leave, on one occasion his sitting down at the piano and singing to his own accompaniment 'Mademoiselle From Armentières'. But what comes back to me most sharply is noticing a peculiar smell emanating from his kitbag and its contents. Not a human smell – I should say now that it was a *chemical* smell, pungent, stale, nasty. I didn't know what it was; in fact it's only when I call it up from the past that I wonder if it could have been a whiff of poison gas lingering in his belongings. (He was never technically 'gassed', with all its lasting horrors of damaged lungs.) Whatever it was, though, I'm certain that if I smelt it again, seventy years later, I should recognise it instantly.

When he was back at the Front, we awaited day after day the postcards he was allowed to send us. They were buff-coloured postcards, presumably issued by the War Department: on them were printed a series of statements, such as *I am well* and *I have received your parcel*, against which the sender was permitted to inscribe ticks. I overheard War-talk about the Great Retreat, the Big Push, and suchlike, without having much idea of what they signified: though I do remember the actual phrases.

Then came a day when the postcards from my father ceased to arrive. I sensed my mother's growing tension without putting two and two together. It went on for weeks, or so it seemed. (He must have been 'missing' without actually being posted as such – separated with two or three men from his battery in the chaos of the Big Push, it afterwards transpired.) There was something ominous in the atmosphere, a feeling that the lives we were living, my mother and I, were somehow suspended. *Then* came another day when my mother, weeping with relief, held a card in front of me for me to read – a tick against *I am well*. Nothing else, but it was enough.

A few months later the War was over and he was back with us.

XIV

From shortly before the War ended I have a most tantalising recollection. It is as if Memory, through being named and ascribed a function, is anthropomorphised into an individual, which, or who, vouchsafes us some recollections and capriciously withholds others. The subject of this recollection is a Zeppelin. I remember being got up from sleep, taken down to the front door, and told to look up at the sky. I can remember that much as if it were only last night. I can see the arch of a starless black sky from beyond the roof of the house across the road to immediately overhead; and I can actually hear a throbbing sound in the sky . . . Yet I simply cannot see the thing itself! Next day we heard where the bombs had been dropped: I can even remember the name of the place, Madeley, ten or fifteen miles away. I am confronted with that great truth: Memory Is A Tease.

XV

After he was back I caught first sight of my father standing on the street corner, waiting to meet me coming home from school. The road on which we lived ran past Crewe station to a small country town called Nantwich: just before it reached us there was a T-junction, whence a road ran down past the school, down and then up again in a switchback over *two* railway-bridges till it reached the middle of the town: there it came to what was once the Market Square but was now simply called The Square, since the market had removed itself to a large building in a nearby street. It was at the T-junction that my father was waiting. Civilian clothes, alert military stance. I felt it was the first time I'd seen him in civilian clothes, in a way almost the first time I'd ever seen him. He hugged me and we walked to the house together. We didn't know each other. He was back. To stay . . .

I suppose that after my father's being absent for four years I might be assumed to have become a mother's boy. I don't recall myself as such. Obviously I was 'closer' to someone in whose company I'd continuously been for four years than I was to someone whom I'd rarely set eyes on for four years; but I have no recollection of being specially accorded or of having specially wanted indulgence by my mother, though I loved her and I'm sure she loved me. What the effect of our 'closeness' was was that I had become conditioned to seeing my father *through my mother's eyes*. It was only after years that I realised this – to my dismay.

On his being established in the house two things were immediately noticeable: he smoked a great deal (a brand of cigarettes called Gold Flake, in bright yellow packets) and he was inclined to be nervous and irritable. My mother's eyes were censorious: he had come back from the War bad-tempered and smoking far too much, she said – and I accepted that, flat, for years. It was only later that I came to notice that she was showing scarcely a glimmer of sympathy for him in the appalling things he'd had to see and to hear and to smell and to do, things off which nicotine might have taken the edge. Little impression was made on either of us by some pencil sketches – he had some gift as an artist – which he brought back with him, pencil sketches I still possess, of trenches, dug-outs, shell-holes, barbed wire . . . but *no* sign of corpses. Although he could refer to them as 'stiffs' and had

17

brought home a splendid pair of Zeiss binoculars looted from one of them, it must have been that he could not bring himself to draw any of them for permanent record. Poor devil! . . .

Bad-tempered and a heavy smoker, my father had come back to live in his own house and to me he seemed a stranger, an interloper, not to say bad-tempered and a heavy smoker as seen by my mother. Instinctively I realised that he was trying to get to know me. (He was an affectionate man.) But it must have been hard for him. However, by this time Ernie had gone and I was companionless at home, which at least may have made it just a little easier for him.

XVI

Resonant with my distress at Ernie's having gone was a sort of gloom which I felt had come to lie over the whole town. The post-War 'flu epidemic – I can't properly recall it as such, can't recall anyone close to us being carried off. Yet a memory lingers unequivocally of a period when, as it were, a heaviness of spirits pervaded the existence of every person, in the houses, in the streets. People were dying.

XVII

My father had begun to teach again. I was now in the 'big school' where boys were separated from girls but taught by women as well as by men. Although my father was one of the men teachers, I have no recollection of being in his class. The class I do remember, Standard III, was that of a youngish woman, Gertie Tipping, plump, lively and silly, lavish with her use of the cane. It is the only class in which I remember being caned, and I was caned frequently by Gertie Tipping – more frequently than the other boys and in my opinion more unjustly. One was caned by holding out one's hand for it. If the cane struck one's hand across the palm it stung and left a weal that lasted for a few hours; if one flinched and drew back one's hand, or if the teacher missed her aim, the cane struck one across the fingers – horrible pain, lasting for days. I thought Gertie Tipping had a 'down' on me, and I hated her for it with a hatred which lasted untempered until I was freed from her by being moved up early to Standard IV. Meanwhile I had come to hate corporal punishment with a hatred that has lasted untempered all the rest of my life. 'Give us a child when it's nine . . . ' Buggered if I will!

Yet I have a comic recollection about corporal punishment. The headmaster used to stalk through the school with his cane under his arm. (A stout length of bamboo.) He achieved an immortal footnote in my family legend, by calling to order the assembled boys of the school first thing one morning – we began by singing a hymn and reciting the Lord's Prayer – with the words:

'You're going to sing " 'Oly, 'Oly, 'Oly",' – waving his cane in the air – 'I'll cut some of you in two!'

The thought of ' 'Oly, 'Oly, 'Oly' raises the question in my mind whether the school had some connection with the Church of England, whether it had once been a Church School. One morning once a week, we, the boys, were trundled across to a religious service in the church across the road. (The clergyman with red hair had by this time gone – who knows where?) Furthermore on the top floor of the school itself, wholly taken up as the boys' domain, there was an intermediate room where the building narrowed

19

between the main sets of classrooms, an intermediate room known as 'The Chancel'. It had a distinctly ecclesiastical look: gothic windows, panelling of varnished pitchpine, and some pieces of ecclesiastical-looking furniture also of varnished pitchpine – a pew and a little desk for praying at. I feel The Chancel must have been reserved to the headmaster himself, though its location ensured that it would be constantly used as a corridor. 'I'll cut some of you in two!' Could that *prie-dieu* have come in for bend-over use at the ceremony of bisection? I never heard any such thing reported by delinquent fellow-members of my class, nor can I remember anybody emerging from The Chancel in two halves, metaphorically speaking. It's just a thought, now.

In fact my recollection of classroom delinquency is that it never reached peaks at which bisection would have been called for. The classrooms, apart from Gertie Tipping's, were disciplined and quiet. We learnt a lot. *Reading*. *Writing*; spelling and grammar. *Sums*; mental arithmetic – I loved mental arithmetic: I knew my multiplication tables inside out. (Having fulfilled the teacher's demand that we should all know the 12-times table, I went on privately to teach myself the 13-times, the 14-times, just for the joy of it: 17 17s are 289 – I can tell anyone that without any thought, should they want to know.) *Geography*. *History*. *Nature Study*. *Science*. I don't regret a minute of it. I was taught. I learnt.

XVIII

I was taught. I learnt. I wanted to *know* things. And it never crossed my mind that being educated was something at which you didn't have to *work* – obviously this was happening long, long before the more enlightened notion came into being, that education might be a branch of the entertainments industry, that *self-expression* should take the place of hard grind. Good God!

XIX

Though the classrooms were disciplined and quiet, the playground was noisy and rough, of course. We played wildly chasing games of Tick; and kicked a ball about, dribbling and shooting in mimicry of Association Football. (I don't think I even heard of Rugby football until a good ten years later.) On the other hand there was a popular vogue for playing marbles, introducing an element of the sedate. I had a collection of polished stone marbles of different colours; grey, greenish, bluish, reddish; and – the treasures of the collection – some glass 'ollies', beautiful spheres of clear glass in which were embedded curving streaks of bright colour. (Also some inferior moulded green glass specimens which came out of the pinched necks of 'pop' bottles, specimens won from inferior boys and not collected by me – class distinction starts in the cradle.) We played the game which I gather is still played in some form or other today. A chalked ring up to which one rolls one's marble in order to land it in the ring or knock other boys' marbles out of the ring. A more aggressive technique than rolling was shooting: one lightly clenched one's fist with the thumb trapped between the first and second finger, rested the marble against one's thumbnail, and then sprang the trap – the marble shot out with deadly effect.

However, the game I favoured most for a spell had a strong 'entrepreneurial' (called thus in order to be in accord with recent improvements in the use of our language) element. It must be the only time I've ever favoured the 'entrepreneurial' element in anything – entrepreneurs, ceaselessly at the ready to take advantage of anyone giving the slightest opening, inevitably strike me as Nature's barrow-boys. For this game one equipped oneself with a piece of wood some eighteen inches long and six inches high, from the lower edge of which one carved out half a dozen marble-width slots, inscribing above them the numbers 1 to 6, taking care to put the high numbers at the ends. One squatted beside the playground wall, set up one's board, and invited all and sundry to roll up their marbles through the slots – paying out the number of marbles inscribed above the slot if a marble went through, confiscating the marble if it didn't. I made a fortune (in marbles). If a boy appeared who was too expert, one simply picked up one's board and went away for a while.

Yet more surprising to me than the recollection of my making a fortune even in marbles is a clear image of my playing marbles along the gutter below the edge of the pavement. It would be suicidal now, yet I'm sure I did it. So sparse and so slow-moving was the traffic, mostly horse-drawn, seventy years ago.

XX

The picture of myself in the playground, withdrawn from the violent hurly-burly going on in the middle of it, makes me wonder if it was then, despite my being only a little below average height and probably better fed than many, that the ridiculous idea took hold of me – a trouble to me

22

later on – that all the other boys were bigger and stronger than me.

So, not only was I tiresomely conditioned in early life by other people: it appears that I was equally tiresomely conditioned by *myself*. (*There's* a phenomenon that I bet the You-know-whos haven't missed out on, either!)

XXI

Cigarette cards. In those days every cigarette manufacturer enclosed in each packet of cigarettes a little pasteboard card with a coloured picture on it. The picture was one of a series – of soldiers in different uniforms, characters from Dickens, British butterflies . . . The cards in each series were numbered, and one's aim was to collect a complete set. As my father smoked so much I had a good start in accumulating a supply of cards from Gold Flake – W. D. & H. O. Wills. Other boys collected, and in a quiet corner of the playground a busy exchange took place in cards of which one had more than one for cards one lacked to make up the set. I don't know if it was the result of the manufacturers artfully printing smaller numbers of some particular cards – in the present day, it could certainly be so, so as to make boys pester their fathers to buy more cigarettes – but in any series there always seemed to be two or three numbers that were rarer than the rest.

The idea was to collect a complete set in pristine condition. With cards that were soiled one played a game, a game of acquisition. Each player held a card horizontally between his forefinger and middle finger and then, with a flick of his wrist, sent it skimming through the air to a chosen spot on the ground; where, if it didn't cover any of the cards already there, it remained; but, if it did cover one of the cards already there, its owner scooped the lot.

But my recollection of cigarette cards is not without significance beyond itself – and I'm not occupying my mind with trifles such as the Freudian significance of collecting, but with something more significant to me. The small cards I have been remembering so far came out of packets of 10 or 20 cigarettes. Boxes of 100 cigarettes contained large cards, and my father sometimes bought, to my mother's disapproval, his supplies by the hundred. There was one series of large cards showing beautiful reproductions of the crests of Oxford and Cambridge Colleges. I fell in love with them. I can still see, for instance, the perfect disposition and colour of the cardinals' hats in the crest of Christ Church, Oxford.

Somewhere along the line of my remembering I've got to try and locate the genesis of my unheard-of intention of going to Oxford or Cambridge University *myself*. Could the seed of that intention to go to one of the Colleges have been sown, when I was nine, ten, eleven . . . by a beautiful cigarette card?

XXII

When I actually was nine a quite different seed was sown, remarkably. A second encounter with the Anglican Church. I was christened!

The event calls for some explanation. My father's family were all Baptists, my mother's all Wesleyans. (On my mother's side there were local preachers and the odd parson; on my father's not, I think.) However, neither my mother nor my father was given to going to chapel, and my recollection of being taken there is solely for 'Anniversaries'. At the date on which a church was founded an annual cele-bration was held, the Sunday School Anniversary. A sort of grandstand was erected at the business-end of the chapel, and on it stood rows, one above the other, of children: the girls were all arrayed in white frocks; I can't remember what the boys wore – if there were any boys. Behind the children stood the regular members of the choir, and the performance consisted of their singing hymns and anthems. I enjoyed it. Otherwise my experience of religious activities was pretty negligible. I was a nicely-behaved little boy, and it was on very rare occasions that I made such a nuisance of myself on a Sunday afternoon as to be threatened: 'If you go on like this, you'll be sent to Sunday School next week!' And on those very rare occasions it never went beyond the threat.

How did I come to be baptised into the Church of England? Well, when I was aged seven my mother and father persuaded me to have piano-lessons. In the big sitting-room there was an upright piano: it had a walnut case adorned by two swivelling brass candle-holders. My mother and father both played a little. I took my piano-lessons seriously even if I couldn't be persuaded to practise enough, and I was taught by the organist of an Anglican church. He came round to the house to give me my lesson, and chatted with my parents. He proposed that I should sing in his church choir, not because I had a beautiful voice but because I could read music and hit the right note – thus giving the lead to boys who actually had got beautiful voices and couldn't hit the right note. (I learnt this later.)

By chance he discovered that I had never been christened.

In the Wesleyan Church I had missed being sprinkled with water when I was a baby: in the Baptist Church I was liable at a later date to total immersion in water – I didn't much like the idea of that. My piano-teacher proposed to my parents that the omission be rectified forthwith by the Anglican Church: they acquiesced, provided that I was willing. By this time I was an enthusiastic singer in the church choir. I agreed to be baptised in the Anglican Church.

I can remember the ceremony. The participants, apart from me, were lined up across the sitting-room, facing the bay-window with the piano behind them. They were my mother and father; a couple, friends of theirs, who had lived next door to our previous house – the house where I was born – and of whom the wife was to be my godmother. (I don't think I had a godfather.) And a clergyman, vicar of the church – it happened to be at the opposite end of the town – where my piano-teacher was organist. I stood facing them, my back to the window, in my hands a prayer-book with which I followed the service.

I feel that water must have been sprinkled on me, but I can't recall the sensation. When it was all over they congratulated me in a general atmosphere of pleasure and affection. I was aware from the ritual that I had been the subject of an unusual occurrence, and I felt rather pleased with myself about that.

Yet about being christened? I had been *christened* Harry Summerfield Hoff. And yet, and yet . . . well, I had always *been* Harry Summerfield Hoff.

XXIII

'*I remember, I remember . . .* ' Not the house where I was born, as I've already observed. But the next house still remains to me the house for fondest remembering. No twee recollections of any '*little window where the sun came peeping in at morn*'; but fondest remembering, for instance of the garden, as well as of the 'big sitting-room' and the coal-house already recalled. It was a long narrow garden divided down its length, between flowerbeds, by three strips of grass, ideal as tracks for racing with my cousin Ernie and later with other boys who came in to play with me after he had gone away. There was a tumbledown disused coach-house at the bottom of the garden, hidden by decaying trees and ideal for games of hide-and-seek. And on the other side of the fence there was the girl next door, freckled, ginger-haired, a few years older than me; a girl whose garden was devoted each year by her father to raising a crop of shallots, from which she broke off long green tops as a delicacy for us to eat raw – a feast immediately detected from my breath by my mother.

Behind the 'big sitting-room' was a big kitchen-cum-living-room, which overlooked the yard and the garden; beyond it, to one side, a small 'back-kitchen', from which an extension comprised the wash-house and the coal-house – the coal-house being entirely visible from the kitchen. (I don't recall what was behind the 'little sitting-room' – the pantry, perhaps. Over each downstairs room there was a bedroom, the bathroom being over the back-kitchen and reached only by going through the 'big back-bedroom'. (I think there must have been chamberpots under the beds –

they were called 'jerries'.) The only heating for all the rooms came from coal-fires, and, because coal-fires cost money and created endless work, a fire was lit in a bedroom only when somebody was ill. So the bedrooms were practically always stone-cold. It was a delightful consolation, I remember, for being confined to bed with some childish illness, quietly to watch the flicker of firelight on the bedroom ceiling.

XXIV

Throughout the whole of my childhood there was never a time when we were without a servant. In an unrelievedly working-class town service was cheap and readily available. I have remarked that Crewe was then, even as it is to a lesser extent now, an important junction of several railways; and it had been chosen by one of the railway companies as the site for engineering works in which to manufacture locomotives. The LNWR, London and North Western Railway Company, plying between Euston and Glasgow: steam locomotives. For its employees the company had built rows and rows of little houses in narrow streets. At eight o'clock in the morning, after warnings first ten minutes earlier, then five minutes, the male populace had to be 'clocking on' at the Works. The summons was by a powerful siren known as 'the buzzer'. Time of day was fixed in the town by it – 'Has the buzzer gone?' or 'Did you set your watch by the buzzer?' I feel that there was another buzzer in the evening, at five-thirty, when the men came out of the Works, to go home for their evening meal. (In the morning they had taken their mid-day meal with them: usually it was gathered up in a big handkerchief knotted at the corners, often a bright red handkerchief with white spots – just before eight in the morning one saw these bright splashes of red among the grey columns of men marching along the pavements.)

The men who were exempted from regulation by buzzer were the aristocracy of railwaymen, the engine-drivers and their firemen: *they*, who were working shifts and had to get up at all hours, were roused individually at those all hours by a company employee coming round to the house and personally hammering on the door – the 'knocker-up' he was called.

In those days the Works were flourishing and I don't think there were many men in the town without a job. On the other hand there were many men, *in* work, who were paid just enough wages to keep body and soul together. It so happens that I saw with my own eyes – I'll come to it later – poverty and near-poverty. (It is only people who haven't *seen* poverty who find it easy not to *think* about it.) Consequently there were plenty of wives and daughters who were prepared to, were forced to, hire themselves out into service. Some left the town to work in the big houses and mansions of the rich elsewhere: others went out daily to houses such as ours in the town. I should have thought that every family above the lowest level of the petty bourgeoisie – and there were precious few in Crewe above the highest level of the petty bourgeoisie – employed a 'girl', as she was called. 'Can you recommend me a good girl? Mine has just left to get married.' In a house such as we lived in, appropriate to somewhere halfway up the petty bourgeoisie, there was plenty of work for a 'girl' who came at eight o'clock in the morning and left at five-thirty in the evening, more than plenty of work in the absence of any mechanical aids beyond a Ewbank carpet-sweeper.

Someone must have recommended to my mother an excellent 'girl'. Cissie was a bit younger than my mother, and she must have come to us when we moved shortly after I was born. (I began by calling her 'Tiddy'.) As well as doing the housework, she became a sort of second mother to me. I loved her dearly, and, when I looked back from some years later, it seemed to me, wrongly, that I had been brought up by Cissie, rather as upper-class children feel, rightly, that they have been brought up by their nannies. It seemed to me wrongly because on weighing it up with more thought I concluded that Cissie and my mother ought to share equally the praise or blame for what might be called the finished result. (A trifling illustration, from when the spot of oil fell out of the aeroplane on to my pram-cover: I cannot say who was wheeling me, because it might equally well have been my mother or Cissie.)

Without effort I can remember Cissie's face, comely and pleasant; more memorable, though, was her speech. Whether it was technically a speech-defect I don't know, but her articulation had a characteristic mushiness – when she pronounced the letter 's' she expelled air from the sides of her mouth as well as from between her teeth. Furthermore 'ck' she always pronounced as 'tt'. The latter was a regular source of fun to Ernie and me. 'What can we have *with* it?' we always asked when presented with a plate of, say, cold beef for our dinner; in order to draw the reply, 'You can have pittled onions. Pittled cabbage. Pittled walnuts. Or mustard pittles . . . ' Needless to say, 'pittle' reminded Ernie and me of 'piddle'.

Cissie didn't leave us when she got married, but stayed with us till we moved to the next house. Meanwhile there was an additional woman to come in every Monday to do the washing – a compelling performance. There was a copper with a wooden lid: it was heated by a fire underneath, and it was a hemisphere not of copper but of a dull greyish metal (zinc?). Sheets were boiled in it. There was a tub, called a 'dolly-tub', and an instrument called a 'dolly-peg', like a small three-legged stool on the end of a wooden broom-handle. The washerwoman put boiling water and soap into the dolly-tub, then put in the washing and bashed the dolly-peg up and down on it. (It can't have done the less robust textiles any good, one thinks – unless one happens to have seen Indian women squatting beside rivers and bashing delicate saris with pieces of wood or flat stones.) The items of laundry were then hung out to dry on clothes-lines stretched across the yard, offering Ernie and me tempting incitement to play catch-as-catch-can in and out of them – until we were noticed from the kitchen window.

XXV

When indulging myself with memories of the garden I remarked that, after Ernie and his mother had gone to live away from us, I occasionally had other boys in to play with me. Occasionally; alas! too occasionally. My mother discouraged it.

'I'm not having them jumping all over the flowerbeds.' Or 'You're not to go and get covered with filth in that old coach-house – and one of you is going to fall down that ladder one day.' And so on.

In the school playground I had made some friends who lived in a nearby street – actually they lived opposite the house where I was born. One of the boys I remember by his name, it was so exotic. Lucien de Wirral. (I hope I've got the spelling right. Fancy a boy being called Lucien de Wirral in a place like Crewe!) He had some brothers and sisters and neighbouring friends: they invited me to go and play with them. I went, and I enjoyed it very much. In due course I was going down to play with them every evening.

'Where are you playing with those de Wirrals?' said my mother.

'In their houses, and gardens . . . ' – with as much conviction as I could find.

'You play *out in the street*!'

'Only sometimes . . . '

'I'm not having you playing out in the street night after night.'

'It isn't night after night . . . '

All the same I thought I had better stay at home for a few evenings.

But the lure of the streets was now in my blood. Playing there was incomparably freer than playing in the garden where the flowerbeds were sacred and the coach-house out of bounds. I began to prevaricate about where I'd been and to invent excuses for being late in getting home. Then disaster!

One evening we were all kicking a ball about in the street and *I* kicked it through the sitting-room window of Lucien de Wirral's next-door neighbour.

Almost before the tinkling of broken glass died away we had made ourselves scarce – I by running back home at full speed. An hour later there was a heavy knocking on our front door. An irate man was holding a ball – it was called a 'sorbo' ball, made of heavy spongy rubber and very bouncy. It was mine. Over what followed Memory is merciful. My father paid for a new pane of glass. 'You deserve a good tanking,' said my mother. (Her word for 'spanking'.) I was sent up to bed. After an appropriate interval for undressing, my father coming upstairs . . .

That was the end of my playing in the street with the de Wirrals. Now forbidden the street and companionless most of the time at home, I awaited with greater excitement the arrival of Ernie to stay with us, and bore his going back home on the verge of tears. I found the prospect of going to stay with him equally exciting, but the parting for me to come home less poignant. In a parting, I now know, it is the one who is left behind who feels the pain of it the more. But these were only visits, interludes, it now dawned on me, in being lonely.

XXVI

The loneliness I recognised may have been real enough, yet I don't recall feeling sorry for myself. Perhaps there was a streak of solitariness in my nature. Anyway, so far as playing in the street went, the veto after disgracing myself with the de Wirrals was not permanent. (Living in our next house, later on, I used to be away from home 'night after night', playing outside with boys who lived nearby – at the age of thirteen still young enough to be rebuked for it, but now too old to be prevented.) In the old house, though, I found consolation in reading. 'Always curled up in a chair with a book' I was said to be; and that seems not surprising, as night after night, i.e. three nights a week at least, Auntie Mag came to the house, where my father set up a folding card-table in the big sitting-room and then he, my mother and Auntie Mag sat down at it to play bridge, a three-handed version called 'cut-throat'. My reading went on against a background of bidding and scoring and discussing afterwards, so boring to my ears that I had no trouble in shutting them to it.

I don't remember what I was reading. Aged nine, ten or so. Was it Hans Andersen, Lewis Carroll? . . . I read them all at some time or other. But I don't recall having read seriously at any age such productions as *Beano*, but I must have seen some of them from time to time: I must have read *Rainbow*, for the name Tiger Tim is still familiar to me, a name so memorable that it would have done credit to Dickens. (Since it must have been pinched from Tiny Tim, I suppose one could say it actually does do credit to Dickens.)

During the years that followed my parents subscribed for a while to Arthur Mee's *Children's Encyclopaedia* for me. I duly read it, opening each new instalment with a lively attention that died away when I had read the pieces that interested me most. Also *The Children's Newspaper*, a nice liberal-minded (as we should now call it) publication – I remember reading in it about The League of Nations. But the time came when my parents saw copies of *The Children's Newspaper* lying around, un-opened. That was that. I regret now that I didn't get as much out of either of them, especially out of *The Children's Encyclopaedia*, as I might have. Perhaps if one or the other of my parents had given a little time in the evenings to proposing that I widen my interests, instead of their being so much absorbed in playing bridge, things might have been different. (I began to hate bridge, and although there was a spell when they tried to teach me how to play it, I'm afraid I'd had enough of bridge before they began.)

There was, however, more exciting entertainment than solitary reading to be had at home. On Sunday evenings we turned round the long sofa in the bay-window of the big sitting-room so that the family and friends piled on it could comment on passers-by.

'There she goes! As usual, head first, tail following.'

'Look at the way *he*'s walking! Is he tiddly, or not quite plim?' ('Tiddly' meant drunk: 'plim' meant right in the head.)

'Now, *she* carries all before her!'

It was often hilarious entertainment, and also, I have since realised, an apt initiation for me into observing people as a novelist might.

But the house was old, and my mother had no use for things that were dilapidating. The crunch came literally. One Sunday evening the sofa, supporting tiers of laughing family and friends, one row of them sitting on the seats and another row behind them sitting on the back, crunched through the floor. For my mother it was incontrovertible reason for moving to a newer house.

This must have been early in 1921. At the time my mother was pregnant again. I can faintly recall her changed shape, the reason for it having been explained to me. After ten years my status as only child was to be ended. Also this was the year when I was sitting a scholarship examination for the local secondary school.

When I was just eleven everything happened at once. We moved house. I had won a scholarship and was ready to start at the secondary school. And my sister was born.

XXVII

Our next house, newer and solider than the old one, lit by electricity whereas the old one was lit by gas, was in a terrace which came next down the road after the secondary school. (This proximity had consequences.) Both the terrace of houses, the houses across the road and the whole of the school building itself were faced with smooth red Ruabon brick: it is difficult to imagine the background for a boy's adolescence being rosier than mine.

The school was called Crewe County Secondary School: the colours black and orange: the school uniform for boys, when I started, short grey flannel trousers – bare knees – black blazer with CCSS embroidered on the pocket in orange silk, black school cap with CCSS embroidered in orange silk on the front. (I'm told the school now calls itself Crewe Grammar School. Indeed!) By the sort of coincidence common to small towns my mother had already encountered the Headmaster in the days when she was a pupil-teacher, and had quarrelled violently, and lastingly, with him. She was afraid now that I should be starting off at the school on the wrong foot. At the end of my time there her fears turned out to have been correct.

On the other hand I myself have never had an overwhelming conviction at any time in my life, either then or now, of being on the right foot. To be on the right foot you have to be in step with everybody else – which seems to me intolerably pedestrian.

XXVIII

Soon after I started at the school my sister was born. I loved her dearly from the beginning. Being eleven years older I was probably as much like a second father to her as a brother. I never remember feeling that she displaced me in the love of my father and mother – they were finding an equal love for her, I thought. Whether she, for her part, felt that I already stood in possession of a love from which she couldn't draw an equal share was something that never occurred to me till twenty years later.

An early recollection of her. A congenital swelling on the side of her face was diagnosed as a naevus and had to be excised by surgery. I went to see her in hospital after the operation. I still remember bending over her cot – our mother was in a bed beside her – and seeing her, the dear little head swathed in bandages, complexion so pale, breathing so quiet . . . Tears sprang to my eyes – they still do when I think of it. Though I had given up the practice of saying 'Gentle Jesus, meek and mild' at bedtime every night, that night I said it again, just in case . . .

My sister lived healthily afterwards and my devotion to her was lasting. In my rôle of second father I taught her to read long before she started school at the age of four. I can still remember my delight and amusement at having her sit on my knee, reading aloud and perfectly pronouncing long classy words whose meaning she couldn't possibly know.

XXIX

Still with my sister in those earliest of her days, I recall a photograph I took of her when she must have been between two and three, sitting in an oval white enamel bath placed on the rug before the kitchen fireplace. The best photograph I ever took. Being taken indoors it was a flashlight photograph, the flash procured by taking a small zinc tray, on the far end of which one had measured out a little mound of magnesium powder; at the near end one placed a lighted match. Tilt the tray – and a blinding white flash followed by a rising pillar of choking smoke. Terrifying to recall!

Everyone who saw the photograph agreed that it was entrancing. (I happened to have got the amount of magnesium powder right, the distances right, the focusing right, the reflecting surfaces – sheets draped over clothes-horses – right, and all the rest of it.) There she sat, my sister, her head and shoulders rising above the side of the bath, her rounded little shoulders beautifully modelled, her head crowned with little wisps of blonde hair looking as if they were alive; and her face . . . laughing delightedly. The only photograph I ever took that I can evoke with pleasure out of memory: the peak of my art as photographer.

Actually my art as a photographer had really begun to fizzle out by the time I was fifteen, when I found myself no longer taking photographs for the fun and excitement of it, but only out of a feeling, increasingly dreary, that I was supposed to be keeping photographic records of things. (Reader: Write an essay of not less than 1000 words on Art and Compulsion!) As a scientifically-minded boy, I acquired at fifteen a 'developing tank' for my films and converted the bathroom into a dark-room for making prints, but I found the fascinations of Technique disappointingly transient. I let photography slide, I'm afraid. I have just the one masterpiece under my belt, as it were. My sister, sitting in the bath, laughing . . .

XXX

The result of the scholarship examination had been announced some weeks before we left the old house, and I was rewarded with my most desired present – a bicycle. My father took on the task of teaching me to ride, patiently running beside me holding on to the handlebars; and once I had responded to the objurgation, 'Stop looking down at your front wheel and look straight ahead!', I was well away. It then took me a little while to pluck up courage to stand on the left-hand pedal and fling my right leg over the back wheel so as to land in the saddle. The reverse action, to dismount, came to me more easily – after all, one was in a stronger position: one could always fall off.

I was ready to go for rides. My father had a bicycle, and he used to take me before school into the country lanes beyond the railway-station, which was where the Marquess of Crewe had a large estate.

By a coincidence the roads round the estate were already known to me. My step-grandmother had a friend, a man about the same age as herself, who owned the largest public house in the middle of the town. He possessed a horse and trap in which he used to take her – and sometimes me – for drives on sunny mornings. At chosen places he would stop to buy fresh eggs, some of which he would give me to take home; and to buy reviving drinks made of hot milk and brandy, none of which he would give me. He was a big fellow, shaped like an egg, with relics of hair combed over his bald head and a rich gold chain stretched across his diaphragm. Among us he was always called Nunkie, and he lived in a big room behind the saloons of his public house: the room was dark and smelt of drink, and the furniture was upholstered with woven horsehair. My memory of Nunkie's sitting-room centres most poignantly in the horsehair on which I was required to sit in my short trousers – woven horsehair under bare knees!

Riding in style, high up in a trap – the other two faced forwards, I backwards – was all very well; but not to be compared with riding my bicycle, my father riding beside me, along these same quiet lanes, again early on summer mornings; the trees waving gently, buttercups and cow-parsley springing yellow and white from the grasses by the roadside, dog-roses and honeysuckle gleaming in the hedges. At one stretch of several miles the estate was marked out from the road by rhododendrons blooming fulsomely in bunches of wine-coloured flowers. Pushing hard up the little hills and free-wheeling down them, my father and I rode in our own style, while overhead there were often larks singing way up in the sky.

XXXI

In honour of our move to the new house, and not without further intentions in mind, my parents had bought a new upright piano. The case was made of dark shining rosewood, and opening the lid over the keyboard revealed an oxidised copper name-plate – CHAPPELL. In honour of the new piano they sent me to a new piano-teacher. It was the beginning of my piano-playing being taken seriously. They and I now realised that playing the piano and playing the organ require different techniques. In playing the organ all you have to do is depress the keys any old how: with the piano it makes a difference to the sound you produce. My father would sit at the keyboard of our new piano, experimenting, listening. 'That's a beautiful tone.' I was taken away from the church organist and sent to the best piano-teacher in the town.

The best teacher in the town was an elderly woman who in her youth had studied 'abroad'. It transpired that she had been a pupil of Leschetizky; who, like Liszt, had been a pupil of Czerny; who in his turn had been taught by *Beethoven* . . . Fancy finding oneself, in this case me, at the end of *that* chain! My teacher still, on rare occasions, gave a public recital in the Town Hall: I shall never forget hearing her play Beethoven's Appassionata Sonata – the first time I ever heard it. And the following year, Chopin's Revolutionary Study. What boy as I was, hearing those two pieces splendidly played, wouldn't want to be a pianist?

My teacher was a big woman, tall and long-nosed, with a boomy voice and a huge beam. Her forehead was broad, her hair looped over it from a parting down the middle; and she had narrow piercing grey eyes – and somewhere on her face a small wart from which grew a single hair (from her nose or chin?). Her boomy voice spoke in an accent which was different from the accent of the town, from the accent of me; and somehow I recognised it as 'superior'. Her hugeness of beam was exaggerated through her being crippled by rheumatism: her public recitals had almost come to an end because it was taking possession of her hands.

I was impressed to the point of being overawed from the moment I first entered the music-room: it *was* a music-room, not just a sitting-room with a piano in it. A large room on the first floor, the walls distempered a bluish green and decorated with pictures whose frames I can see glimmering in the lamplight – I must have gone for my lessons in the evening. Pictures of composers, Mozart, Haydn, Schubert: a white plaster bust of Beethoven. The floorboards were exposed, polished and creaking, with a few rugs lying here and there. The light, the only light, came from a strong lamp beside the piano. There were piles of music, a music stand and, I think, a big vase of dried flowers. The piano was a small grand piano.

No music-teacher could have had stronger views about

41

the difference between playing the organ and playing the piano. Whatever her technical inheritance from Leschetizky – even via Czerny from Beethoven – she was now a devotee of the technique known as the Matthay Method. The method as such is long out of date, and I suspect that Tobias Matthay was a bit of a crank. Nevertheless, nowadays when I'm watching pianists in close-up on television, I find myself looking to see if they produce the force for depressing the keys by using the flowing weight of the arm and the body as well as from the muscular thwack of the fingers and wrist – and feeling a spurt of academic disapproval if they don't.

I became absorbed. Playing music began to give me a sort of happiness, of consolation. Only since I've been adult have I realised that 'curling up in a chair with a book', or constantly playing, even practising the piano, are common resorts of children who feel lonely, not easily bound in with their fellows. There were signs that I might be embarking on a musical career.

My mother and father took such signs seriously. I gather from Margaret Drabble's biography of Arnold Bennett that *his* parents diagnosed him quite early as an artistic child, without having any idea what form of art he was destined to practise: I think *my* parents may well have felt the same about me, and I suppose I did myself; only in my case all three of us thought the art in question was music. Ten years later all three of us turned out to be wrong.

Meanwhile, although I was no longer having piano-lessons from the church organist, I still sang in the church choir. The church was inclined to be High. There were a fair number of candles flickering, a fair amount of what my mother called 'bowing and scraping' – people crossing themselves, nodding their heads, even genuflecting – but no incense, no thurible-swinging . . . Medium-High, perhaps? Following a man carrying a polished brass cross we boys led a procession in pairs up the aisle, being thought by nearby members of the congregation to look angelic. In the pockets of our cassocks were secreted sweets which, under cover of our surplices, we passed from hand to hand and then popped into our mouths when the organist was not watching us through the mirror above his keyboard.

I think we all enjoyed singing, especially when, on the third Sunday of the month, Matins was replaced by Sung Eucharist – Sung Eucharist gives you something to get your teeth into. At chosen high spots in the calendar we performed an oratorio. I feel I've always known Handel's *Messiah*, yet it's the less superior Stainer's *Crucifixion* and Maunder's *Olivet to Calvary* that I remember singing. I particularly enjoyed a chorus in the former – 'Fling Wide the Gates!' – the injunction reiterated in a couple of rousing arpeggios up the notes of the common chord. A fine opportunity to fling wide the larynxes!

XXXII

Eleven years old, twelve . . . Puberty was 'raising its head' – what a beautiful ambiguous way of referring to a beautiful *un*ambiguous object, which I discovered what to do with, entirely on my own, through the concurrence of chance and instinct. I must have had it in my hand when I was kneeling one summer evening at the wide-open window of my bedroom, gazing idly across the 'allotments' and fields. Suddenly I chanced to see in the distance a couple of frisky dogs, one mounted on the other excitedly thrusting to and fro . . . Instinct, before I knew what was happening, had taken over – bringing me shortly to the most dazzling discovery of my life. 'Instinct and Chance in the Human Predicament' – what a marvellous theme for a major novelist!

XXXIII

Crewe County Secondary School took both boys and girls, and looking back I conclude that a school for both sexes nicely accommodates the vices of two-sex schools and the vices of one-sex schools as well.

Shortly after I began there, the wings of scandal circulated a riveting story. A Sixth Form boy had been caught actually doing it in the chemistry lab with a girl identified as the Headmaster's daughter! The youth was expelled on the spot, the girl silently eased out at the end of the term – *noblesse oblige*. Then there was the continuing gossip about one of the Sixth Form boys paying regular visits to one of the schoolmistresses. I knew him, a tall, dark-haired youth, more mature-looking than most. It happened that the schoolmistress lived in a house across the road from ours and when I went into our sitting-room after school to practise the piano, I quite often saw him presenting himself at her front door, carrying his books – he was going for extra tuition. No wonder he looked more mature than most.

Up to the Sixth Form, boys and girls attended class separately. Boys and girls had contiguous asphalted playgrounds, opening on to a common playing-field, where there was a football pitch for the boys and a hockey pitch for the girls. In the winter I always had chilblains on my toes which caused me excruciating pain to put on my boots, let alone to kick a football. (If I did manage to squeeze into my boots and put in an appearance on the field, when the two sides came to be picked for a game I was naturally one of the last to be called.) And in the summer, for fear of getting my piano-playing hands injured by a cricket ball, I chose to play tennis – there were two hard courts in the schoolyard. So, whether I was solitary by nature or not, I missed team games entirely. But the playing-fields gave everyone, however athletic or unathletic, scope for other activities Such as making arrangements for assignations in the evening.

I was one of a party of boys, when we were around fourteen years old, who got caught up by a party of four notorious girls, two of whom were sisters living where the edge of the town gave way to fields. We used to assemble a little way beyond their house and they led us rambling over the countryside in the evening light. Little hills and valleys, clumps of trees, brooks trickling fast, a mill-pond somewhere . . . And the girls' *pièce de résistance* for entertaining us? A recital, chanted rhythmically in unison, of all the dirty words they knew –

'*Dash, darn, bugger, fuck, damn!*'

I don't remember how it went after those first five most memorable of words, but I do remember how excitingly shocking it was. (Nowadays when women-novelists establish their parity with men-novelists by writing dirty the way men write dirty, the shock is totally lost on me – I've known for sixty years that they had it in them to do it.)

Among the four girls it was the elder of the two sisters who allured me most. She had carmine cheeks and narrow brown eyes. I think she was the original inspirer of the rhythmic recital, a poetess in the making. Much more

45

to the point, though, was the fact that she wore an exceed-ingly close-fitting navy-blue skirt below which she displayed sturdy, shapely calves at rest: but it was when, seen from behind, she *walked* . . .

Towards the end of those evenings, when the twilight was deepening, I would draw the carmine-cheeked sister apart from the others (who were also drawing apart in pairs) for the purpose of heated kissing and fumbling. Uninstructed kiss-ing and fumbling . . . Exciting, pleasing, satisfying after a fashion. *She* seemed happy. *I* knew, from the theory of it all, that this was not the end of it: what I lacked was knowledge of the practice, i.e. what to do next, how to get *out* of the repetitive sequence of uninstructed kissing, tentative fumb-ling. I wondered if, compared with the other boys, I was a slowcoach. How was I to tell? 'Uninstructed' was the key word. I had come up against what I was dimly beginning to realise was a serious flaw in my temperament. Child of peda-gogues, I wanted to be *instructed* in things first of all.

When we, the boys, were on our own there was no lack of knowing conversation about sex. Knowing, yet not explicit – certainly not explicit enough for me. The only pedagogical instruction in the subject that I had ever received came from my mother, delivered at the earliest age – when I was being bathed, I think. The most grotesque piece of *mis*instruction. Never let anyone touch my sexual organ. Misinstruction impressed into me so deeply that it took me years to root it out. (When I did root it out and made a start, well! . . .) So when the other boys engaged in knowing conversation I felt left outside it; because I didn't *know*. I did my best to follow without being exactly sure what they meant. Too proud and shy to disclose my ignorance, I had to pretend.

Among ourselves we paired off as friends on no very conscious basis. I paired off with a bandy-legged youth who came in from the country: what we had in common was the highest regard for each other's randiness, calling each other 'Prick' and 'Wire' respectively. In rough-housing we grabbed at each other's genitals – it was known as 'knacker-fighting' – and in class surreptitiously signalled below desk-level the present degree of our randiness. It came as a surprise to me to hear later on that a couple of pairs of youths I knew as friends had been in the habit of retiring to the long grass at the top of the playing-field, there to discharge their heatedness in each other's company. I concealed my surprise. And I was also told about an older bull-like boy gathering together a circle of other boys in the playground urinal and showing the biggest John-Thomas they had ever seen. I hadn't been invited to the display. Always outside the inner circle of things, I . . .

A present-day journalist would unerringly entitle my account of adolescence *Autobiography Of A Slow-Developer*, to which I could add the subtitle *Or Things I Have Missed*. I suffered the disadvantage (to last for half a lifetime) of looking younger than I was. Furthermore I was innately shy of 'group activities', in fact I evaded them. I did not join the Boy Scouts: I deplored spending weekends in accumulating badges to sew on the sleeves of one's shirt. (It was only when a boy in my Form, who lived down the road from us, was sent home from camp with swollen testicles – his mother told my mother – that I had any idea of what the Boy Scout Movement could really mean.) And on Friday mornings the school day began with 'Drill' – a sort of poor man's OTC – when masters who fancied themselves in command ordered ragged lines of boys to march up and down the muddy playing-field. As there was no roll-call I simply stayed at home and played the piano. I wasn't missed. As time went on I sometimes extended the evasive tactic, made easy by living so close to the school, to lessons given by masters I didn't think much of. Obviously there were *some* inner circles I didn't mind being on the outside of.

XXXIV

In the evenings after school things were different. Our terrace of rosy-bricked houses had small back-gardens, which opened on to a cinder-track wide enough for carts delivering coal and collecting rubbish. And on the other side of the track was fenced off a substantial area comprising narrow strips of ground where local residents cultivated vegetables – these were the 'allotments'. (Beyond it was the school playing-field.) A locale altogether ideal for boys' games, of which the favourite was called 'Bobbies and Burglars' (subsequently Americanised into 'Cops and Robbers'). There were half a dozen adolescent boys living in our terrace of houses, some in the next terrace, some a little way off, so we usually had a fair quorum of players. In and out of gardens, over walls and gates and fences, up and down the allotment paths we went. Out 'night after night'. Of course we were out at night: that was when the game was most exciting – the bobbies had torches with which to hunt the burglars hiding in outhouses and behind walls and under bushes. My parents totally failed to keep me indoors and had to reconcile themselves to my coming home long after dark, dirty and sweating, with my clothes said by my mother to be 'ruined'. I realise this doesn't fit in with my picture of myself as always outside the inner circle of human fellowship: in fact when I was playing 'Bobbies and Burglars' I felt gloriously one of the crowd – and I *was*.

We had some less rumbustious pursuits. One was a game played on a summer's evening when there were only two of us out. Each of us purloined from home a reel of black cotton and went out into the road, where we squatted on the pavement, one against the wall, the other opposite him at the edge of the pavement. We then went through the motions of winding thread from one reel to the other, and when passers-by approached we asked them if they would mind stepping over our thread. To see adults cautiously trying to negotiate a barrier that was not only invisible to them but to our knowledge non-existent was a source of delight and astonishment to us.

Another quite different pursuit introduced elementary technology in the shape of a rudimentary 'telephone'. A boy who lived a couple of houses away, and occupied a similarly sited back-bedroom to mine, joined forces with me in stretching between the two houses a length of twine, at each end of which, below the window, hung a tin can, through a hole in the bottom of which the twine was threaded and knotted. By pulling the twine taut, speech uttered into one tin can could be heard in the other. It was an exciting thing to have available, but as it incorporated no summoning device it could only be used by carefully timed prearrangement – when we might just as well have said to one another what we wanted to say without using our telephone. So it came to be abandoned as ultimately impractical.

This reminds me of another ultimately impractical piece of technology. A bizarre and foolish incident happened on one of Ernie's visits. He shared my room, and one night we were sitting on the edge of the bed in our pyjamas, talking around an obvious topic. (It seems that boys of thirteen must be in a state of arousal half the time.) The thought occurred to us

– suppose we had wet dreams in the night, what about our pyjama trousers? Discovered in the morning! We cogitated: and then one of us, I can't remember which, had a brilliant idea, so brilliant that I should naturally like to claim it for myself. It was to use a sponge-bag as overnight protection – made of a rubber-backed material, with a draw-string round the top, what better? Ernie's own sponge-bag, in which he had brought his toothbrush and face-flannel, lay on the washstand within arm's reach. (In those days, though everyone used the bathroom, the bedroom furniture still included a marble-topped stand, on which the centrepiece was a large china bowl with a large empty china jug in it, along with an unused china soap-dish and an empty carafe of drinking-water.) It was a perfectly good, even brilliant idea; but a preliminary try-on by experiment showed us, alas! that it, too, would be ultimately impractical.

XXXV

However, other recollections from the age of thirteen, on a thoroughly different line, enable me to establish what I like to think of as a moral balance, if not to figure as one of the most admirable and priggish boys. I didn't join the Boy Scouts; I evaded Drill; I did a bunk when lessons came up from a master I didn't like or didn't think much of; but I chose to make a most important gesture towards conformity.

At the church where I sang in the choir I was marked out by some higher authority as a potential acolyte – a 'server' as it was called – at the Communion Service. I was very pleased to hear it, though it would mean my cycling down to the church on a Wednesday morning before breakfast in order to function at the 8 a.m. celebration. When I came in due course to performance, I enjoyed it very much; moving to and fro reverently, bowing, genuflecting, crossing myself exactly on cue; helping the priest with this and that. I'm afraid I have to admit that I wasn't strongly aware of the presence of Our Lord, but that was no doubt because at the most critical moment of His presence I was required to go out and pull the church bell three times, so that devout members of the congregation who had elected to stay in their beds could be with us in the spirit.

But before I embarked on this modest career of acolytry, I had passed my next turning-point, the third of my encounters with the Anglican Church, that move towards being on the right foot – *Confirmation*! Demonstration, if not proof, of my afore-mentioned moral balance.

I had become mildly friendly with a boy in my Form who lived near the church and attended it regularly: he was religious in a giggly way and was already thinking of becoming an Anglo-Catholic clergyman. It may have been that in conversation with him the subject of confirmation came up – he was confirmed at the same time as me. I have a vague recollection of rather perfunctory confirmation-classes before choir-practice on Thursday evenings; but the only detail that remains clear to me is a preoccupation with the opening question and answer in the Catechism.

'What is your name?'

'N. or M.'

I have never known either then or now what N. or M. stand for. 'Norman or Margery', for instance? I can't believe that. On the other hand I am not going to dispel the poetic quality of my ignorance by 'research'.

The climactic evening dawned. There were lots of

lighted candles at the top end of the church: my parents, staunch non-Conformist non-chapel-goers, were loyally present among the congregation. And the Bishop of Chester officiated in full regalia. I *think* I remember his laying his hand on my head. So I was confirmed, signed and sealed into the Anglican Church.

In itself it had been a stirring ceremony. When we got home my father said:

'Well, lad, how do you feel *now*?'

I didn't answer. I was thinking about it.

I finished thinking about it. I had no answer.

Something or other was supposed to have descended upon my head along with the Bishop's hand. The fact of the matter was that I didn't feel at all that anything had. I felt exactly the same as before.

XXXVI

Signed and sealed into the Anglican Church, I – descended on my father's side from good Baptists, on my mother's from good Wesleyans. (Always referring to them as 'good' Baptists and 'good' Wesleyans is a habit I picked up from my mother. The appellation was tinged with an irony on her part which has, through the years, faded from mine. Good Baptists, good Wesleyans – why not? They probably were good.) Which thought impels me to summon up remembrance of families past . . . I will begin with my Baptist paternal grandfather.

If my earliest of recollections begin with a sight of one of the first aeroplanes to fly over Crewe, a recollection from not much later counterbalances it with a sight of one of the last horse-buses to travel the streets. I was not in a pushchair, so I must have been about four: I was standing in a side-street in Crewe, and I have an image of a horse-bus travelling slowly past the end of the street, along the main street which had been named, with reverence appropriate to its period, Victoria Street – in 1914 the great Queen had been dead only thirteen years. The town's park was called Queen's Park. I remember seeing, in the shop-windows in Victoria Street and elsewhere, souvenirs, especially mugs, still carrying the portrait of Her Majesty, a heavy checked old lady wearing a widow's cap with a small coronet on top of it. The side-street, off Victoria Street, where I happened to see the horse-bus, a double-decker with the top deck open and reached by a spiral stair, happened to be the side-street where my paternal grandfather lived.

Horses were of course at that time being replaced for traction by internal-combustion engines, the new buses being called 'motor-buses' to distinguish them from their predecessors. Cars were always called 'motor-cars' by us. Motor-buses were coming in: but for the early years of my childhood – for instance at the time when I was playing marbles along the gutter – most of the traffic was horse-drawn. People came out of their houses and shops with shovels and buckets after horse-drawn vehicles had passed by, to collect the droppings as manure for their gardens – as my step-grandmother did. The droppings left a pungent whiff in the street, and in cold weather they steamed.

Before motor-buses for the public, motor-cars were making their appearance for private citizens. The family living across the road from us in the old house owned one, promoting an early induction for me into awareness of social standing. Their house was bigger than ours, detached, with a tennis-court beside it. The father was a professional man – there were a few such in Crewe – perhaps a lawyer, anyway of social standing higher than that of elementary schoolteachers. They had a couple of daughters aged twenty or so, one of them fascinatingly called Weeda. (It was only when I became A Man of Letters that I realised Weeda must have been Ouida.) We exchanged 'Good morning!' with each other across the street, but I scarcely remember our going into each other's houses: their 'Good morning!' was uttered in a different accent from ours, which I some-how knew to be – like my music-teacher's in later years – superior.

What do I mean by this 'superior'? How and why did I come to recognise it as 'superior'? Silly question – every Englishman and woman knows the answers without asking the questions. They come ingrained beyond experience or reason. By the time we left the old house Weeda's father kept a motor-car permanently just outside the house, and their friends arrived by motor-car to play tennis. An induc-tion for me into the desirability of higher social standing.

So much for free associations stirred by the horse-buses and the motor-buses of the period. Now is the time to get back to family history, to the side-street where my paternal grandfather lived, to my paternal grandfather himself.

XXXVII

My paternal grandfather was a painter and decorator. In the side-street off Victoria Street the front part of the house was a shop, with wooden racks up the walls for holding rolls of wallpaper. Beside the shop was a narrow passageway, an 'entry', at the end of which, adjoining the backyard of the house, was a long warehouse where the men who worked for my grandfather – I remember there being three or more – kept their ladders and planks, trestle-tables, paint-pots and buckets.

My grandfather's name was Arthur, his wife's name Abigail: their children, of whom there were six, in maturity irreverently called them Charty and Ab, and claimed, with anecdotes to substantiate their claims, that their father was born idle. At this time he must have been in his late sixties; he was short, with an old man's little dome of a pot-belly; his head was bald with streaks of grey hair combed across it. He wore a pair of steel-rimmed spectacles, and a straggling grey moustache which did nothing to conceal or enhance the appearance of his false teeth. To get about from one place where his men were working to another he rode a bicycle which was painted silver – it was to be seen leaning against the wall at the bottom of the entry. Having been in his youth, according to his children, the very skilful rider of a 'penny-farthing', he had celebrated his advance to equally skilful performance on a modern machine by painting it silver. As an alternative to being called Charty he was also known at home as The Silver King. (I understand this was the title of a popular play.)

My first recollectable sight of my grandfather – I don't suppose it was my first actual sight – is on entering the living-room from the shop, a dark living-room with only one small window high up in the wall; and coming upon him lying on his back on a sofa, the little dome rising in a mound from his middle, an open newspaper spread over his face. Beside him, for the time being swivelled away from the sofa, was a little wooden bedside-lectern on which was an open book. (The lectern had been designed and constructed, I was told, by my grandfather himself, to save the trouble

55

of holding the book while he was lying down reading it.) At present, on this my first recollectable sight of him, the newspaper spread over his face was moving gently with the rhythm of his snoring.

I registered this pleasing restful sight independently of such anecdotes as I had already heard about his idleness. The one most favoured among his children was of his sitting at the tea-table beside his wife, and while touching the handle of the teapot with his forefinger, saying:

'Pour me a cup of tea, will you?'

And yet, and yet . . . In due course I learnt that he was an energetic regular conductor of the Town Band. (His silver-topped baton is now inherited by the one of his great-grandchildren who has become a professional musician.)

There was plenty of movement in the entry, on the part of his men carrying ladders and paint-buckets and suchlike to and fro; but not on the part of my grandfather. I never saw him doing any painting and decorating, with the exception – here comes another countervailing anecdote! – of the particular painting at which, with universal acclaim, he excelled. He was an artist so unusually skilled that he got special commissions from miles around – to do oak-graining on doors. When he was doing it he comported himself like a true artist, skilfully, carefully, thoughtfully, absolutely seriously; standing back from time to time to study and appreciate the effect.

The process began with the application of a lightish base-coat of paint; then the next darker coat flicked on with a brush called (if I remember rightly) a 'flogger', giving a surface covered with little ticks of paint; finally a top-coat, allowed nearly to dry, and then streaked into the graining and knots with a comb. Sometimes to get a softer graining effect, he covered the teeth of the comb with a bit of cloth, and sometimes for the knots he used his finger covered with the cloth. Time was no object: what mattered was the intrinsic beauty of oak and the verisimilitude of the final work. The final work of art. My paternal grandfather, painter and artist.

The other thing I recollect about him – another source of fun to his children – was that he had a mania for installing doors; for instance, from the entry into the backyard he had installed two contiguous doors, one or the other entirely unnecessary. There were further examples inside the house, such as an entirely unnecessary door at the foot of the staircase. Comical but very odd – what would *his* analyst have said?

During the latter part of my paternal grandfather's life I had picked up references to the present financial circumstances of the family, something to do with going bankrupt. It was not until after his death that I was told by my mother, she presuming, I imagine, that I was now old enough to comprehend the irony of it, that he actually had gone bankrupt: he had gone bankrupt as a consequence of doing a vast amount of work for the Baptist Church – for which he was never paid. Poor old Charty! Idleness may have been in his genes, but life's experience cannot have given him much encouragement to break out of his genetic inheritance.

Abigail, on the other hand, was the opposite of idle; nervous, jumpy, inclined to be frenzied. She had a squarish sallow face, with a small nose and small brown eyes. Her house-cleaning was thorough to the point of going beyond a mere inclination to frenzy. Her idea of cleaning a room was to begin by throwing everything out of it. (If that was in *her* genes, I can only say it was a gene that was transmitted to me. I find myself doing the same, to the jeers of *my* family.) I think the justification for throwing everything out was to get at the carpets. There were no vacuum-cleaners in those days, the only way to clean a carpet thoroughly, more thoroughly than the dust-raising mode of brushing it *in situ*, even if sprinkled with damp tea-leaves beforehand, was to haul it out of doors, hang it over a clothes-line and beat it. There was an instrument sold for this purpose: on the end of a longish handle was a flat head made in a pleasingly-designed open weave of bamboo strips. Sold for the purpose and given by God to express my grandmother's frenzy. Abigail's family made regular fun ot it.

'Where's Ab?'

'Out in the yard beating the carpets!'

Fun so regular that I'm persuaded that my first recollectable sight of her was beating the dust out of a wretched carpet suspended across the backyard. (There was no garden to speak of, so the backyard offered plenty of space for the operation. And her backyard, like my step-grandmother's, was paved with glossy bricks of that memorable slatey-blue colour.)

Now a recollection of her on quite different lines – she had a passionate taste for Thomas Hardy's *Tess Of The D'Urbervilles* and George Eliot's *Adam Bede*. I remember those two novels coming into her conversation often – not any others so definitely, though just possibly now and then one of Charles Dickens's. As I hadn't read either *Tess Of The D'Urbervilles* or *Adam Bede* at the time, it is only by the effort of recapturing in memory the tone of voice in which she spoke of them that I can distinguish a difference in her feeling towards them: she sympathised deeply with Tess, of course; yet she really loved Adam. Good for her! I say, now that I have read the books myself.

Abigail's maiden name was Adams, and in the matter of what serious writers with a sociological bent call 'ethnic origins', she was said to be a mixture of Welsh and Liverpool-Irish. Having been brought up on the Borders of Wales myself, I had been duly fed with an appropriate ration of the local 'race-memory'. And what did my local race remember? Randy little Welshmen, covered with red hair, coming down from the hills and robbing them of their cattle and their wives – to put both to the same purpose, perhaps? . . . And the Irish? It may be that the Irish working-class don't universally enjoy the highest social prestige; in Crewe the Liverpool-Irish were literally at the bottom, nobody lower. So much for Granny Hoff.

The 'ethnic origins' of Grandad Hoff are more obscure. There was a family myth about it. Now one of the charms of a myth is that it's obscure; another is that it's implausible. The family myth was that the name was Dutch, and the first of my traceable forebears to carry it came over from the Low Countries as batman to an English officer at the end of the Dutch Wars in the eighteenth century. A detail added to the story, no doubt to reduce its implausibility, is that this *ur*-Hoff came from Vriesland – thus pin-pointing our place of origin.

As a consequence of a university friend of mine, his curiosity provoked by the uncommonness of my surname, taking the step on his travels of searching for it through European telephone directories, I learnt a few years later that Hoff occurs in small numbers in all the countries bordering the North Sea. Another friend, at about the same time, preparing to write a book on the Pilgrim Fathers, came upon it as the name of a passenger in one of the little boats crossing after the *Mayflower* within the following years when passenger-lists were still kept – a Hoff coming from

There was a tragedy in my Auntie Ede's life. I listened to her singing in the sitting-room. In the kitchen there was a perambulator in which always lay a baby, my Auntie Ede's little daughter, with hydrocephaly. The huge head, with the silkiest of fair hair and blue veins beating at the temples below, the finest of complexions . . . When I went to look at her I felt shy, distressed, and in a shameful way repelled. I remember it very clearly. She died a little while after her father came back from the War and they went to live outside Liverpool; and my Auntie Ede's story changed to happiness in the end, when, after waiting five years or so, she had another baby – a fine, strapping, healthy boy. The little girl's hydrocephaly, my mother told me when I was old enough to understand the facts of parturition, was the result of an incompetent forceps-delivery at birth. I recall the occasion of my being told as the first time I was confronted by the appalling things people have to put up with sheerly through the turn of fate.

The eldest sister, Auntie Nell, plays only a small part in my memories. She was married and lived in Hoylake. She was regarded as rather bad-tempered, and I think my father had quarrelled frequently with her, as well as with his brother Fred, when they were young. She and her husband didn't appear very often at the family home. An eccentric pair. They had no children; he worked in Liverpool and had not gone off to the War. (As I write this now, I begin to realise, as I had not realised so sharply before, that a man who had fought in the Great War enjoyed a prestige not enjoyed by a man who hadn't: and in the scale of prestige, having fought in Flanders stood higher than having fought on any other Front.)

The chief source of joy for my Auntie Nell and her husband – and the chief source of amusement for the rest of the family – was their ownership of a motor-cycle and side-car. The comicalness of my uncle's appearance in his motoring-goggles was easily eclipsed by the comicalness of Auntie Nell's appearance in the side-car, which was made of wicker and shaped like a Bath chair. When they exchanged the motor-cycle and side-car for a little motor-car with only three wheels, known as a Morgan Runabout, their comicalness was not reduced, since they saw fit to install their dog, a huge animal with hair all over its eyes, in the seat over the single back wheel, whence it barked continuously at the top of its voice wherever they went.

Actually Auntie Nell and her husband did have me to stay with them three or four times while I was a schoolboy. The thing I remember about their house is that in the sitting-room there was a pianola, at which my uncle, having fed into it a roll of strong paper patterned with perforations, sat pedalling away while a dazzling piano-performance, determined by the perforations, echoed round the room. Seeing myself as a human pianist I privately took a very high line about the sound of mechanical music, and only very reluctantly responded to their invitations to play the machine myself. Happily they took my *hauteur* as shyness.

Not far from their house was the famous Hoylake Golf Course and from time to time they took me for walks across it – on one occasion with my father, who was a golfer, I even played a round on it. It was subsequently renamed The Royal Hoylake, presumably by persons oblivious to the sound of two 'oy's on top of each other. Royal Hoylake, indeed!

XXXIX

On my mother's side family connections were much more sparse. The central figure throughout my childhood and boyhood was my step-grandmother. She it was who, according to my mother, consistently 'spoilt' me. In my mother's attitude there was an element of objection to my being 'spoilt': in my own attitude there was not. When I was about fifteen I decided to call my mother and father Edith and Ernest – I can't think what started me off, unless it was reading in my step-grandmother's *Daily Sketch* about the provocative antics of the 'Bright Young Things'. (It was 1925.) It was a bit of a shock to my mother and father – it was unheard-of in our sort of family – but they settled down to it and in due course were not, I fancy, averse to it. When I decided to go one better by calling my step-grandmother Mary Elizabeth, the shock all round, especially in the case of my step-grandmother herself, was more enduring. She was very affectionate, and not very bright, and I doubt if she ever got used to it.

To place Mary Elizabeth as my step-grandmother – and to explain much else – I shall have to tell the story of my mother's early life, here pieced together chronologically from bits of it that she told me from time to time during my adolescence. A story beginning in 1886, when she was born. Her mother contracted puerperal fever. And died.

XL

My mother's mother was a country girl, daughter of the village blacksmith in a Cheshire hamlet not far from Crewe. Her name was Cooper. A Wesleyan family. From childhood she and a boy called Summerfield, son of another Wesleyan family, who owned a flourishing ironmongery business in Crewe, had been sweethearts – 'neither of them had ever looked at anyone else'. The time came and they married; a blissful union . . . And then the appalling turn of Fate happened to them.

I am able to recall with gratitude and affection that my own mother and father unfailingly did their best for me, made me aware of their loving me, and gave me a happy childhood. My mother's experience was utterly the reverse; a lifelong memory of what had happened to her unfortunately coloured, it seems to me, everything she recollected. Having before me the example of being brought up to see my father only through my mother's eyes, until years later when seeing him through my own eyes I began to see something different, I have constantly to remind myself that I am seeing my mother's early life through her eyes only, have no means of seeing it through my own. I can easily imagine that the sudden death in childbirth of his passionately loved wife temporarily unhinged her father's mind: it is a shocking thing to imagine, though it appears to be not uncommon, that he blamed the child for her mother's death and found himself unable to stop himself venting blame on the child herself.

My mother described to me acts of cruelty from her

babyhood, at least one act of physical cruelty. It may even be as well that after a short time her father abandoned her to be reared, under the eye of relations, by foster-parents in the countryside around: none of them, according to my mother, was kind to her. Meanwhile her father, back in his ironmonger's shop, took heavily to drink.

The next step was when her father decided to marry again, presumably in part to set up a home for his child, in part to reclaim himself from drink. (Among good Wesleyans, drinking was a sin.) Against the advice of his family he married Mary Elizabeth. Now Mary Elizabeth was a very affectionate woman but not very clever; and it is possible that about her affectionateness there was something clinging and cloying. She adored her father. He kept a jeweller's and pawnbroker's shop in a street nearby. She had always lived at home. After only quite a short spell in the ironmonger's shop, she went back, taking my mother with her – back to her father.

At that my mother's father gave up altogether and disappeared from the town, never to be seen there again. Actually he is supposed to have been heard of, by chance much later, in a town somewhere in Lancashire, living with a 'wife' and children. He was never divorced from Mary Elizabeth, so I speculate on the existence of a covey of unknown Summerfield relations of illegitimate birth – a peculiarly appealing speculation, as the family myth on my mother's side is that Summerfield derives from Somerville in Norman times. Our country abounds in bastard Norman blood and it is nice to think of Summerfields, all good Wesleyans I hope, adding to it.

Incidentally I should remark that the family is Wesleyan because John Wesley preached in the house of one of them and converted them. Be that as it may – it's more plausible

than that Vrieslander-batman story on my father's side. My
mother's father was not seen again and the ironmonger's
business was taken over, with great effectiveness, by the
husband of his sister Sarah, who appears later in my story
as Great-Aunt Sally.

There is no evidence that Mary Elizabeth was anything
but kind to my mother, nor was Mary Elizabeth's mother
– 'an old besom!' according to *my* mother – and Mary
Elizabeth's two brothers, also watchmakers and jewellers.
(Mine appears to be a family pullulating with watchmakers-
cum-jewellers.) They made my mother feel that she was
not wanted – and this feeling of being 'not wanted' must
have been ingrained beyond reprieve. I will pick up the
recollection, later, that she gave me the impression, at one
time – at *one* time, I repeat – of having married my father,
who fell in love with her when they were schoolteachers
together, partly in order to get away from this home.

XLI

So there was Mary Elizabeth living alone behind the
shop, her mother and father long dead, in the days
when she 'spoilt' me. I remember her friendly smiling
face having rather amorphous features, the amorphousness
of her small shapeless nose being increased by her nervous
habit – made fun of by us – of constantly rubbing the end
of it with her fist. She was usually dressed in black, down
to the ankles, with a gold watch hanging on a chain over her
chest and the neck of her dress filled in with what she called
a 'front', a sort of fine muslin bib (in colour ecru, a shade of
fawn), which had a high stand-up collar stiffened by strips

of whalebone. Over the dress she wore in winter a knitted multicoloured woollen waistcoat known as a 'hug-me-tight'. On her feet high-legged boots – pairs of boots done up with buttons which she fastened with a button-hook.

Thus I remember her from quite soon after the time of my second-earliest reminiscence, of falling out of my pushchair in her backyard. The backyard was overlooked by a large square bay-window in the living-room/kitchen, the bay being filled by a most enviable collection of aspidistras along the side of the dining-table. Opposite the table was a resplendent small kitchen-range, the cast-iron ovens and fire-grate gleaming with energetically-applied blacklead, the bevelled edges of the steel hobs polished to the brilliance of silver – even the walls of the recess in which it was housed were blackleaded. On one side of the fire-grate was a large oven for cooking, on the other side a small oven for heating water. Around the hearth was a fender of brilliantly-burnished steel-plate, perforated in an elegant design: and in front of the fender a hearth-rug the like of which I have never seen since – composed of rectangular strips of rag stitched to some sort (possibly hessian) of backing, black with a central diamond-shaped inset outlined in red and pale-coloured in the middle.

As the only other apparatus for cooking was a single gas-ring in the back-kitchen – the house was lit by gas – it was over this range that my step-grandmother did practically all of her cooking. As I recall, joints of meat roasting in the oven; potatoes, vegetables, boiled puddings, cooking over the fire; sauces simmering on the hobs . . . Marvellous feats, Mary Elizabeth was achieving, in that simple English cuisine which tends to be one of God's most unappreciated gifts to our beloved country.

We went to Mary Elizabeth for mid-day dinner every

Sunday, and it was the meal of the week. (I have to remark that my mother was an equally good cook in the same genre, but with her the delicious dishes were spaced out through the week, while at Mary Elizabeth's they all came at once.) Nobody could beat Mary Elizabeth in roasting a piece of sirloin; with its juice beginning to ooze out while she cut the first slice, revealing a fine outer ring of crisply-browned fat, shading to the most succulent of red meat in the middle. Perfectly roasted potatoes, creamily mashed swedes, airy slices of Yorkshire pudding . . . Nobody could beat her in roasting a chicken, either – its skin layered in the early stages with slices of bacon, part of the stuffing (made with marjoram in preference to thyme because of its blander flavour) cooked inside it, part outside in little balls baked to a brown crustiness; and bread sauce, of course. Sometimes cabbage or sprouts, so carefully steamed that anyone who turned down the boiled version of them in a restaurant would have accepted them here with pleasure, savouring the white sauce with a touch of nutmeg in it. I could go on. Her roast pork – the crackling, the gravy, the stuffing made with onions and fresh sage. Veal with little rolls of bacon, stuffing like that in her chicken, and white sauce incorporating chopped hard-boiled eggs.

At Christmas Mary Elizabeth always roasted a goose, slowly for hours, beginning with the whole bird enveloped in a pastry-case which was removed at a later stage so that the skin reached a most edible degree of crunchiness. (Carefully she collected the oil which came out of the goose – it comes into my story later.)

And, oh! Mary Elizabeth's puddings. (I can't stop!) She favoured no short cuts or economies in preparing the Sunday dinner. For instance, custard, whether baked or boiled, was never made of anything but eggs, numerous eggs – I still can't help looking down on Bird's custard, even though some people say they prefer it. The custard was served with puddings. There were sponge puddings, mainly baked, one containing ground rice and having a layer of jam underneath; another with a layer of jam on top, covered over by meringue; another incorporating scraps of lemon rind and served with lemon sauce. And – only too rarely to be come by nowadays! – delicious steamed suet puddings, light as can be, with golden syrup poured over them; or containing marmalade and having marmalade sauce poured over them; or made like Swiss rolls with jam in them and jam sauce poured over them. Oh, the beautiful past!

Having made preparations galore the previous evening, Mary Elizabeth took it as a matter of course that she would spend the morning entirely on her cooking singlehanded. (On Sundays the servant, who did the housework and helped in the shop, had her day off.) We were required to be on parade at 11.30 a.m. So the Sunday dinner was over by half-past twelve. It was followed by a ritual appearance at the back door of a poor old former retainer, come to carry away a Sunday dinner that would serve her twice if not three times. Dressed in a Victorian bonnet and cape, she always unlatched the back door with the opening line –

'Amma too soon?'

We used to wait for it; in fact we got so used to calling her 'Amma too soon' that I have a job to remember her real name – I think she was 'Old Mother Payne'. Sitting on a little table just inside the back-kitchen door she regaled us with weekly news from a grandson who was serving his country in Chittagong.

Mary Elizabeth made the marmalade and jam, of course, and lemon curd. It was she who made our 'pittled onions, pittled cabbage, pittled walnuts and mustard pittles'. Furthermore she had a speciality in wine-making – elderberry wine, dandelion wine, rhubarb wine and coltsfoot wine. Coltsfoot was her favourite, and she used to take me trailing across nearby waste-ground, scouting for the flowers, little cups formed by a ring of many, many tiny yellow petals, not too easy to seek out among the big dazzling dandelions. The wines were brewed in grey stone jars tapering under a brown glaze to the mouth and the handle. When the string round the cork was unwound the cork shot out with a wonderful pop, so something must have been going on in the jar's contents. To my chagrin I can't recall the flavour of those clear golden liquids: all I know is that they were sweet and warming. (Perhaps I should remark that drinking home-made wines was much less reprehensible than drinking beer or spirits.)

XLII

In order to find me an occupation for dull Sunday after-noons, Mary Elizabeth inducted me into the art of cooking. I can't say I had two specialities, as this would imply that they were two confections which surpassed several others. They were in fact the only two: one was toffee, the other gingersnaps.

The gingersnaps I made were never what I was aiming at. I realised much later that what I wanted to make were brandy snaps – shiny, sticky, brown, rolled into cylinders, with an inconsistency in texture such that in the thinnest spots they were almost transparent. Our recipe was for ginger-biscuits, cut out with a tumbler into flat khaki circles of uniform opaque consistency – very edible but not what

I wanted. A total misfire in mutual understanding between me and Mary E.

The toffee, on the other hand, was generally a success; made simply of butter and sugar, which I weighed out on Mary Elizabeth's scales with the polished brass scale-pans and cooked over the back-kitchen gas-ring in a polished brass saucepan. The prime danger, which I didn't invariably avoid, was taking my eye off the saucepan in the last moments and letting the toffee burn. The tricky bit was assessing when it was cooked, determined by dropping a little drip of the molten toffee from a spoon into a cup of cold water, where if it was not cooked it formed a sugary mass dissolving into the liquid around it, while if it was cooked it could be hooked out as a satisfactory hard blob of toffee – and the rest of it promptly poured into a shallow flat tin, to set. (It was while the tests were going on that the toffee in the pan might burn, making a fearful smell as well as wasting precious butter and sugar.) Even so there was a variation in the product, from the hard and brittle to the sticky and chewy: both were acceptable, and sometimes I put in black treacle, as a consequence of which the toffee was bound to be sticky and chewy. (I feel that there were still further variations, in which I incorporated almonds or walnuts.) Toffee-making was an engrossing Sunday afternoon activity, warding off all threats of my being sent to Sunday School – I suppose I *was* making a nuisance of myself, but Mary Elizabeth took the strain of it.

XLIII

However, for being 'spoilt' it was spending a weekend at Mary Elizabeth's which set the standard. I was put to sleep in a featherbed so downily deep that it was like a nest: there was a fire in the grate if the weather was in the least cold, and a stone hot-water bottle at my feet if it wasn't. My breakfast was cooked especially for me when I saw fit to get up: the rind and bits of bone were of course trimmed off my bacon: if I was offered a boiled egg, the top was lifted off for me: my round of toast, having had the crust removed, was cut into three or four slices for me. And as I didn't drink tea, I was given a deliciously nourishing cup of milky Cadbury's cocoa – which sounds nauseating to me now but which I savoured then.

Mary Elizabeth was expert at dressing a crab, and for me she not only cracked the claws but extracted the meat. The same with lobster. Shrimps were usually potted; but if they were unpotted she shelled them for me. The same with prawns. (I still refuse to order prawns in a restaurant if I'm expected to shell the wretched things for myself.) So far as I recall, I never peeled an orange or an apple for myself at Mary Elizabeth's.

Of course there were dishes that Mary Elizabeth liked that I didn't. I remember her tucking into pigs' trotters, cow-heels and tripe – not for me! The brains of some animal or other cooked in a white sauce I quite liked. And I liked very much sweetbreads fried with bacon. Above all her cooking of calves' liver with bacon, in a succulent brown sauce containing onion and parsley – for me, every time!

While indulging myself in this orgy of culinary reminiscence, I simply must, out of truthfulness, record that after a weekend at Mary Elizabeth's I often had a bilious attack: my mother thought it served me right, but I thought it was worth it – and nothing my mother could say would stop Mary Elizabeth's 'spoiling' me. Not that my mother herself didn't take extraordinary care of me, to say the least of it. I remember being dosed with a strength-giving medicament called Virol, a sticky malty substance of honey-like consistency; and horrid cod-liver oil supposed to ward off colds; and if I actually had been ill, a delicious meaty sort of jelly called Brand's Essence spread on wafer-biscuits. Furthermore, as if this were not enough, Mary Elizabeth, a convinced believer in homoeopathy, dosed me when she thought it was necessary with an assortment of little white pills called Nux Vomica, Camomilla, Bryonia and others whose names I don't remember. By great good fortune I had been born with a constitution which enabled me to survive both foods and medicines.

XLIV

I think I must have been about thirteen when my interest in Mary Elizabeth's business really sprang to life, possibly because I began to be allowed to take a hand in it. The establishment was situated on a street-corner. There was a front-shop and a back-shop. In the front-shop were sold secondhand articles which had not been redeemed from pledge; in its main-street shop-window were sold men's gold watches (normally worn in the waistcoat pocket), gold chains (normally stretched from one waistcoat pocket to the one opposite), gold 'alberts' (the decorative object which dangled from the middle of the watch-chains), and occasionally wristwatches; women's watches (rather fewer), gold chains and wedding-rings; in its side-street window were chiefly firsthand merchandise such as sheets, blankets, towels, some articles of women's and children's clothing, aprons, bars of soap. (It was on these windows that I was allowed to make my first (and last) essays in window-dressing – I still remember the Parthenon-like structures I composed with bars of soap.) In the back-shop, entered more privately from further down the side-street, was the pawnshop, above whose door hung the famous sign of three golden balls. That was where I got my most fascinating view of life, and where in my boyhood I came face to face with poverty and near-poverty.

All the customers in the pawnshop were women, mothers and wives. I don't remember ever seeing a man there. (If a man for some private reason had to come in himself to pawn something, usually his watch, he came into the front-shop.) The mothers and wives were poor, many looking underfed, dressed in shawls to keep them warm because they lacked overcoats; yet for the most part they were lively and talkative and generally honest. (There were a few given to sharp practice but Mary Elizabeth kept an eye on them.) They brought in men's suits, men's pairs of boots – Mary Elizabeth didn't think much of women's shoes – and assorted shirts, blouses, shawls, petticoats, men's thick woollen vests and long underpants. And they brought them in and took them out, alternating working-clothes with 'Sunday-clothes', for most of the time according to a basic routine: for the beginning of the week they redeemed working-clothes and pledged 'Sunday-clothes', for the end of the week the reverse. On each transaction of redeeming they paid interest according to the size of the loan and the length of time the articles had been in pledge. Over and over again for the same articles.

When I got a bit older I longed to say to these women:

'Don't you see, if by hook or by crook you can manage without the money for just one round, you needn't get into this routine at all?'

A boy of my age, with no part in the business, couldn't put that question to them of course; and I realised that I should probably be met with incomprehension if I could – their mothers and grandmothers had been doing it for as long as they could remember. One saw newspaper articles making a case that the working-classes were improvident if not of low intelligence. These women were not without native intelligence and were trying to be provident; it was by the incessant, grinding struggle to keep going at all, I thought, that they were too borne down to *think*.

Of course there were cases outside the routine, a sudden emergency in a family, such as an illness which demanded the immediate finding of money to pay medical bills (no National Health Service then!). A woman would come in with every dispensable article in the home, including her wedding-ring. Now I come to think of it, wedding-rings, gold wedding-rings, came in quite often – such probably being the most, if not the only, valuable articles in the home. Mary Elizabeth was pretty sharp in assessing the value – 9 carat, 11 carat . . . If she were uncertain she telephoned for the advice of her elder brother, whose jeweller's and watchmaker's shop was the foremost in the town. (She telephoned by means of a private line: to use it one lifted a receiver off the top of a box on the wall and summoned her brother by giving a few sharp turns to the handle sticking out from the side of the box.)

Although there was always a 'girl' who worked in the

shop, as well as in the house, Mary Elizabeth herself always did all the valuing of goods brought in for pawn – brought in for the first time, that is. When they were brought in for a second time or more, the girl was sometimes allowed to handle the transaction: the customer told her the previous valuation and she would hand out the money – which gave a fly pledger the chance to tell a sum considerably higher than the original valuation.

With Mary Elizabeth herself I remember very little argument or pleading for a higher valuation: she had years of experience and of reputation for being fair. She was on friendly terms with most of the regular customers who, presumably in the Victorian tradition of referring to the pawnbroker's as 'Uncle's', often called her 'Auntie'. To many of them she behaved, in her good-natured, affectionate way, rather like an auntie, helping them out when they were in serious trouble – helping them out not in the sense of over-valuing their pledges or reducing the interest, but of giving them discarded clothes and bed-linen or offering them remedies for illness. She was particularly noted for her stocks of oil which came out of the Christmas goose when she roasted it: all over her parish 'Auntie's' goose-oil was rubbed with sovereign effect every winter into the chests of children suffering from bronchitis.

The women brought in their husband's suits and pairs of boots unwrapped: along with the articles of clothing they were expected to bring a piece of cloth: after valuation the articles were wrapped in the piece of cloth and thenceforward known as a 'bundle'. The transaction was recorded in a ledger and a ticket was issued: the ticket was perforated, one half being given to the customer, the other half pinned on the side of the bundle. (The pins were especially large and strong, 'pawnbroker's pins', immediately identifiable if they found their way out of the shop into the drawer of a sewing-table.) The tickets had a different colour for each month, beginning with white for January and running through the glowing gradations of the rainbow as the year passed. The part of the business I was duly permitted to take a hand in was making entries in the ledger and writing out tickets, and on Sunday afternoons counting out the contents of the till.

Upstairs, in a small bedroom, suits were lined up on hangers, boots in rows on shelves: that room had a stale smell. In pigeon-holes in a big bedroom, and in a large shed outside in the garden, and in the shops themselves, the bundles were stacked by the month, all the blue tickets shining together behind their pins, all the orange, all the red and so on. The faint smell was, I now think, probably of the soap in which the contents had been washed – the soap I had arranged with innate architectural skill in the shop-window. Sometimes there was a crisis when a bundle could not be found: perhaps it had been misplaced or the ticket had been carelessly pinned on; or, worse still, some customer, while Mary Elizabeth's back was turned, had managed to steal it from one of the racks behind the counter.

There were other, more human emergencies, for instance a sudden knocking at the back door, long after the shop was shut, on a Saturday night – an agonised woman whose husband had just come home from the pub and was furious to discover she had failed to get his Sunday suit out of pawn. The quarrels there must have been off-stage! From confidences between 'Auntie' and customer, Mary Elizabeth had a shrewd idea of which wives were beaten by their husbands. I was too young to understand.

Outside business Mary Elizabeth had other preoccupations. Her serious study of homoeopathy was one. She believed that Nux Vomica was a cure for bilious attacks, and she administered it to me. (However, when I stopped going to stay with her for weekends, I was never bilious again.) Studying spiritualism was another. She went to seances and took a magazine called *Two Worlds*. By now becoming a devotee of H. G. Wells, I was unimpressed by the contributions of Sir Arthur Conan Doyle. Photographs of ectoplasm, people apparently spewing out white-of-egg, seemed to me only too easy to fake. And I'm afraid I began to tease her about seances. When for instance she came back from one in October with a few scraggy chrysanthemums she'd found in her lap when the lights went up, I said I should believe they came from another world if they'd been daffodils.

Over Sunday dinner we used to ask her if the spirits had given her any messages for us. She had a planchette board, but it never yielded any message remotely comprehensible – the spirits saw fit to favour *us* only with incoherent hieroglyphics. (This was in the days long before incoherent hieroglyphics could be construed as messages from the Unconscious or regarded as manifestations of High Art.) However, one day she came back from a seance to divulge that *I* was being directed by an Indian Guide. Thinking she meant a brown Indian from India – a shrewd, clever little man, I visualised – I was not displeased. I shall never forget my consternation when I discovered she meant, of all things, a Red Indian. Hiawatha . . . Heaven help me!

Mary Elizabeth lives in my memory, but the pawnshop no longer exists: no longer do the three balls over the side-door glimmer with gold like the domes of the Vatican and the Kremlin. Those were the days before 'easy' loans, hire purchase and unlimited credit facilitated living without money in the present, at the expense of putting off the evil day of paying till some unnamed date in the future. Pawnshops have gone, thank goodness! The rich have found other ways of squeezing the poor.

XLV

Mary Elizabeth lives in my memory, and for more than twenty years after her death I treasured a solid memento of her good nature – a gold wristwatch, just out of pledge, that she gave me on my eleventh birthday, to set me up in my new life at the secondary school. Mary E. knew a good watch when she saw one, and in any case she could call for the advice of her brother, 'our Charlie'. The watch has kept faultless time over a period so long that I can still see it as it was when I parted with it as a present to one of my own children. A leather strap many times renewed, a squarish gold case with a dent at the bottom right-hand corner, a chip in the white enamel face between two o'clock and three. It carried me through secondary school, university, years of career. It was merely out of vanity that I parted with it in favour of a more up-to-date-looking specimen – to see it treasured and still worn today by my child because it was a present from me. Dear Mary Elizabeth, darling daughter!

XLVI

Crewe County Secondary School and the expanding world
of adolescence, of finding things out, of learning things . . .
At home I had already embarked on an expanding range of
hobbies – determined by instinct or chance? Chance, so far
as I can see – what else could explain rearing butterflies,
for instance? At school on an expanding range of subjects,
determined without any either/or by the NUJMB, i.e.
Northern Universities Joint Matriculation Board.

I had begun the school-year at CCSS just after my eleventh birthday and was due to take School Certificate four
school-years later, some weeks before my fifteenth birthday.
Mathematics, Physics, Chemistry, English (Literature and
Essay), French, German, Geography and History – I think
that was the tally of subjects. If one did well enough in the
School Certificate examination one was awarded Matriculation, so I was told. Thus 'Matric' was something to be
striven for; but what on earth it signified nobody ever
explained. Just strive for it, was the rule.

Over recalling the tally of subjects I have what might
be called a problem. Religious Knowledge. I know I didn't
take it in the examination; because I remember the offence
done to my susceptibilities at being required to take seriously
all the implausible stuff in the first books of the Old Testa-
ment. From my reading about evolution in *The Children's
Encyclopaedia* I gathered that there was a rational account
which left no place, let alone need, for allegory, myth or
suchlike about how the world (and we) came into being. I
was beginning to have intimations of what I came to think

must be one of the deepest instincts in my nature – it *must* have come with the genes – to put my trust in rationality, in the method of scientific enquiry. If RK was originally on my list, I must have found some way of getting out of it.

I remember the lessons in Geography, because the master was a short, irascible fellow, having a strong right arm with which he dealt out crashing blows to the heads of stupid boys. *Not* a master for me. I studied how to do a bunk from his class without detection: home I went for half an hour's respite at the piano.

English lessons were a different matter. My response to them I can only describe as pretty well all-round resistance, alas! We were taught some grammar and spelling, for which I am grateful. I'd had a good grounding in spelling at the elementary school, but I appreciated more of it. I liked learning things, getting them right. In the lessons on grammar I thoroughly enjoyed Parsing and Analysis, for instance: I experienced pleasure every time I saw how the bits of a sentence were assembled in order to make sense, especially to make sense gracefully. But when it came to reading 'set books', things took a turn for the worse. I realised it was not the English master's fault that we were forced to read a protracted rigmarole about Amyas Leigh; and another master-work about a Crusader, over which Memory has cast a Veil. In the case of another book, about a character called Girt Jan Ridd, the attention of the whole class did suddenly spring to life – sniggering life, I have to admit – when he is exhorted –

'Git up, git up, Girt Jan Ridd.'

A moment of delight for thirty boys.

But the main cause of my resistance, which I now realise was regrettable, although I should be dishonest if I said I regretted it inside the next twenty years, was that I disliked the English master from the beginning and hated him towards the end. He was energetic and noisy, one of the masters who chucked his weight about in the so-called Drill sessions on the school field every Friday morning. A bushy black moustache and a big nose, a big red nose. He was called Bodge by us. I thought he was coarse. (Coarse-fibred would be a more accurate description, but I didn't know the word then.) Finally he offended me beyond repair.

He set us to write an essay on crime and punishment. (No connection with Dostoievski's novel, which we knew nothing about.) Now my juvenile view – and I wish I could say I'd changed it all that much in maturity – of The Essay was that it's something you write, or worse still are required to write, when you haven't got much, if anything at all, to say. It's possible, just possible, that what I wrote at Bodge's command about crime and punishment was tinged, just tinged with the provocative. When I got the essay back he had written at the bottom –

'If this is what you believe, your spiritual experience must be very shallow.'

My second thoughts were that he might have been nearer the mark had he said my spiritual experience was not so much shallow as non-existent. To be succeeded by final thoughts that perhaps *both* were wrong.

However when I first read his comment – even though I had asked for it – I was furious. So far as I was concerned, that was the end of diplomatic relations with Bodge. (When the results of the School Certificate examination came out I had credits in English Literature *and* English Essay.)

The lessons I remember most vividly were in German. We were all taught French as our first foreign language, and anyone who was good enough at French was allowed in the next year to choose between Latin and German as a second

language. Obviously German – no Dead Languages for me!
(It served me right: I had to learn some Latin later in order
to get into the university.) I liked learning German, as I had
liked learning French. The German teacher was a delightful
woman. She was middle-aged, friendly and conscientious,
and she was a *lady*. Now it's arguable that for a woman
teacher to keep order in a roomful of lower-class boys and
girls, it is better for her *not* to be a lady. (As the number
of pupils taking German was small the class combined both
sexes, but it was the boys who made the running.)

Miss Fox-Davies was a lady, well connected I afterwards
learnt, rare . . . Her hold on discipline was tenuous to say
the least of it. No opportunity was missed, especially by
the boys in the back rows, to take advantage of her. She
habitually wore plain cashmere polo-necked jumpers, which
of course revealed to our eyes a pneumatic presence above
the waist. And she had a gold watch, hanging from a very
long gold chain, which she kept *inside* her jumper.

'Please, Miss Fox-Davies, will you tell us the time?'

This immediately let loose speculation about where
the watch was hanging in the first place, followed by avid
observation of its being hauled up through the gap between
the hills. Universal hilarity.

Worse was to follow. In the room there was a piano at
which Miss Fox-Davies sat down to accompany us in singing German songs. (She really was a good, decent teacher.
We, I'm afraid, were neither good nor decent.) The German
songs – 'Die Lorelei' and so on. Preferably and so on to
'Ich Hat Ein' Kamarade', in which the comrades keep in
step, 'Schritt und Tritt'.

'Please, Miss Fox-Davies, may we sing "Schitt und Titt"?'

And – 'Oh, *why*, Miss Fox-Davies, can't we sing "Schitt
und Titt"?'

I feel very ashamed when I think of it. Cruel, mannerless little members of the lower orders we were.

I can only say, by way of mitigation, that I worked very hard at the German language. When it came to the examination I began by writing down, at great speed on a separate sheet of paper, a chart of all the declensions of nouns and adjectives, singular and plural in all the cases; thus I could check that in my answers I had got all my case-endings right by just a glance at it. I had a pretty fair stock of irregular verbs. And I could rattle off prepositions in lists according to the case they took. (Rattle off to this day: *aus, ausser, bei, seit, mit, nach, von, zu* take the dative, of course. A piece of knowledge of permanent use, I'm sure – it could easily get one out of a tight corner in Frankfurt or Bayreuth.) And a final stroke of swottishness, I made myself expert in German handwriting, and in the final examination used it for all my answers in the German language. I was very disappointed at getting only a Credit and not a Distinction in German – until years later, when it occurred to me that I might have struck an examiner who, either having forgotten how to read or more likely never having learnt to write *Deutsche Handschrift*, couldn't make head nor tail of a quarter of my papers.

I ended up with Distinctions in four subjects and credits in the rest. Distinctions in Mathematics and Physics for certain; and, I have a feeling, in History and Geography as the other two. Not in English, of course; but I wouldn't have minded one in Chemistry and would definitely have liked one in French or German. However, only one boy did better, with five Distinctions, the boy who practically always came top of the form – I was always second or third. I was not especially narked by his always coming top, as I thought he was a dull dog, cut out to end up as manager of a local bank. What I *was* especially narked by was my mother's nagging:

'You're not going to let *him* beat you again, are you?'

(The latter narking turned out to be not so much single-edged as double-edged, when I realised, a few years later, that *au fond* my mother would have been relieved if I'd shown signs that *I* was cut out to end up as manager of a local bank.)

Having got my School Certificate with Matriculation thrown in I was ready to move on to the Sixth Form, where one had to specialise; to *tak' the High Road or tak' the Low Road* to a steady job if not Fame and Fortune – in other words, to take 'Science' or take 'Arts'.

XLVII

Earlier on I thoughtlessly disclosed that I reared butterflies, which sounds a pretty eccentric hobby – not the only one, either. Looking on them now, I feel I could say that what they had in common was a biological bent to begin with, and later a physical – in any case not 'on the Arts side' of things.

In rearing butterflies I remember each stage well; first caterpillars, then chrysalises, then final transformation, final transfiguration to beautiful powdery-brown creatures with blue roundels on their wings. But Memory will vouchsafe no information about where I got the caterpillars from. Certainly I didn't collect the eggs; nor did I go round the garden catching any caterpillars I happened to see – proved by the fact that *all* my butterflies were Peacocks. I feel I must have bought the caterpillars through seeing them advertised in some magazine or other; which sounds in modern circumstances a bit out-of-the-way. I kept the caterpillars in a shoe-box, feeding them with leaves of, I think, silverweed. (*Something* I fed with silverweed: I used to go out looking for it, a low-growing plant with frondy leaves a rather dim green on the upper surface but underneath a shining silvery-white.)

My mother did not much approve of my box full of caterpillars, crawling up the sides, and I took great care that none of them escaped – she was constantly on the watch for anything which might 'make a mess' about the house. When they turned into chrysalises I transferred them to matchboxes, half-opened and up-ended with the chrysalises hanging from the roof.

Then came the day of heavenly transformation, heavenly transfiguration to the delicate creatures with roundels on their wings. I fed them, newly-born, from a blob of honey on the end of my finger, and they soon got into the way of fluttering down for it, consuming the honey by unrolling tongues of quite extraordinary length. A recurrent delight to me, to see them come fluttering down.

But then came another day, when my mother said:

'Isn't it time you let those things go?'

It *was* time . . . I waited for a sunny afternoon and suffered a sad moment of parting when they finally rose from my finger and fluttered away.

XLVIII

I reared frogs. I know where I got *them*: I went the rounds of local ponds with other boys collecting the spawn in jam-jars. When the spawn turned into tadpoles I fed them with 'ant's eggs', dried brownish little objects the size of a match-head. And when the tadpoles sprouted legs I transferred them out of doors to a shallow rectangular stone kitchen-sink, half-filled with water and tilted so as to provide a patch of dry land at one end for them to climb on to. Tiny frogs – steadily decreasing in number as they grew big enough to hop out of their home. The first year I expected the garden to be alive with full-sized adult frogs. I never saw any. Did voracious birds sweep down and eat them? I never saw that happening. Or did they starve to death? I never came across a single corpse in the flowerbeds. A mystery.

XLIX

All this rearing of Nature's lesser creations began when I was eleven or twelve, and went on till I was fourteen or so. (I hadn't realised till now that I was ever interested in pets.) We had a canary. His cage hung in a bay-window in the kitchen, and when we opened the door he flew round the room. My mother rapidly wiped the picture-frames on which he had alighted – for once she was willing to put up with the 'mess'. He would perch on her hand and she was fond of him. On one occasion, when she thought he seemed unwell, she gave him some diluted brandy – and came back half an hour later to find him hanging from his perch upside down.

For me there was some fun in the bird's bursting vociferously into song whenever I started to play the piano two rooms away.

L

I remember other pets. Rabbits and a dog. On no account to be reared in *our* house. I never thought of asking for rabbits; but I did broach the little matter of a dog.

'I'm not having any dog making messes all over the carpets when it's a puppy; then leaving dog-hairs all over the place when you've trained it.'

So who kept rabbits and a dog for me? Why, Mary Elizabeth, of course.

Our venture into keeping rabbits began with a contretemps. Mary Elizabeth permitted the two animals to mate, and then, when parturition was due, segregated them. Unfortunately the one which was supposed to be the doe lived in solitary style in its hutch, while the one which was supposed to be the buck had a clutch of baby rabbits in the open. The affair was a bit outside my province at that age, but how could Mary Elizabeth have made such a mistake? Does it throw some light, I wonder now, on a nature which led her to end her married life so soon and go back home to her father? Is that too far-fetched an idea? Yes. Anyway, after the contretemps things went well. We reared dozens of little rabbits: they were easy to dispose of among the women who came to the pawnshop. I did not dwell on the question of what was to become of them after that.

The dog was a success. I contracted to exercise it on Saturdays and Sundays, and that was all the claim that Mary Elizabeth made on me – my mother thought I had an easy time of it. I chose the breed of dog myself. Mary Elizabeth had a passion for Yorkshire terriers, and there was always one about the house, taking possession of the ancient most comfortable rocking-chair by the fireplace, a pretty little creature with sweet silky hair and a snappy little bite. I wanted something that was more of a man's dog. I chose a Cairn terrier. Naturally I wanted a pedigree animal, and to this end I studied a journal called *Our Dogs* and answered advertisements I found therein. (It occurs to me that I must have read some pretty odd journals.) Why did I choose a Cairn? It embarrasses me dreadfully to record this, but it would be cowardly of me not to. I had read in Mary Elizabeth's *Daily Sketch* that Cairns were a breed favoured by Edward, Prince of Wales.

LI

Another odd journal I remember was called *Rover*. I remember because I was forbidden by my mother to buy it. What moral deterioration she thought it might initiate I cannot now imagine. Anyway, I bought it and hid the copies under the mattress of my bed. I read them at night under the bedclothes by the light of a torch. I found the boys' adventure stories moderately exciting; but what I really wanted was the series of glossy black-and-white photographs, given away each week, of Football League teams.

Why did I want the photographs of football teams? I was not particularly interested in the performance of the teams

– I was no student of League tables. I don't think it was a matter, as it had been in the case of my collecting cigarette cards, of emulating and competing with other boys – I don't remember other boys collecting them. As I recall, it was an entirely private thing. I wonder now if it nurtured some vicarious sense of participation in the game with the heroic players photographed, remembering that I was debarred from participating on the school playing-field by horrible chilblains on my toes. A sign of something? Who's to say?

Sheerly as a spectator of the game, however, I did enjoy being taken by my father to watch the local football team play on a Saturday afternoon. The team was called Crewe Alexandra – known as The Alex. When I now see *Match Of The Day* on television I'm stunned by what a marvellous game Association Football is. But my enjoyment of the games my father took me to watch was somewhat dampened by the fact that The Alex always seemed to lose the match – so regularly that when nowadays I see the football results come up on the television screen, I can scarcely believe my eyes when they convey the news that Crewe Alexandra has won!

LII

Having declared that all my hobbies might be classed as 'on the scientific side', I promptly remember one that claims to be counted 'on the artistic side'. Embroidery!

My taking up embroidery resulted from falling off my bicycle. Something of a fashion sprang up among us thirteen-year-old boys for trick-cycling – freewheeling with one's feet on the handlebars, or kneeling on the saddle,

or paint – 'still lives', such as a jar with two or three paint brushes standing in it and a pair of spectacles lying beside it, or a pile of books and an apple. I was not bad at Art.

But what irrelevantly springs to my memory at this moment is that the corridor outside the Art room, being isolated from the rest of the school, was frequently the scene after Art class of some tremendous knacker-fighting.

LV

So much for my hobbies 'on the artistic side'. With them I should like to count in – I think I must count it – my musical studies, making the point, not in any specially carping sense, let me say, that in the whole caboodle (one of my father's words) I was never confronted with the existence of the possibility of original composition, of 'creation'. Oh well, I suppose I got there in the end – or rather found myself there.

LVI

Throughout this period my cousin Ernie and I were still exchanging holidays with each other as a regular thing. When I was staying with him one of our favourite excursions was to travel to and fro across the Mersey by ferry-boat. After breakfast Ernie's mother gave us the fares and some sandwiches, and off we went, out of her way for the day.

For me those early views of the river were hyper-romantic.

I remember them perfectly. The glistening ripples on the surface of the water, the slow passage of the ships nearby, and finally, in the distance, rising above a summer morning's haze, the twin towers of the Liver building, the shine along the gilded wings of the liver birds on top of the towers growing brighter and brighter . . . In my memory now I see it like a Turner painting. When we arrived at Liverpool we strolled along the wooden landing-stage towards where the great Cunarders with their red funnels, the White Star liners with their white funnels, were roped to the quays while people busily moved up and down the gangways.

Sometimes on other occasions we went, usually with our mothers, on another ferry to the seaside resort at the end of the Wirral peninsula, New Brighton. There there was an ironwork tower like a smaller version of Blackpool Tower, both inspired by the Eiffel Tower. To us it stood for the excitement and fun of a holiday. (No wonder!) Though I haven't been to New Brighton since those days, I gather that the Tower stands there no more.

Two of the ferry-boats we travelled on were called *Iris* and *Daffodil*. The names were enshrined romantically in my memory from the beginning – and revived in it with startling resonance when I read of their heroic part in ferrying to safety relics of the defeated British Army from Dunkirk in 1940. *Iris* and *Daffodil*, I knew them both. Fancy them being *there*!

Why my exchange of holidays with Ernie petered out I still cannot tell entirely. We changed from little boys into youths, no longer each other's *alter ego* as differences in our natures, just as differences in our bodies, asserted their rule over us. He grew taller than me; and I now feel pretty certain that he matured earlier – not that I set him much of a pace in that respect. Yet I still don't remember any quarrels or disagreements or noticeable dying away of friendly emotion. It just began to happen. An active part in its being snuffed out was played by my mother. My mother decided that she was having Ernie to stay oftener and for longer periods with us than his mother was having me to stay with them.

This was not an unusual manoeuvre on my mother's part. I was not, or felt I was not, encouraged to bring home my schoolfriends; but I have to admit that inviting other boys in one's Form to one's house was something that nobody else seemed to go in for, though I should have liked to. (It was rare even for boys who lived nearby to play in each other's houses, when we could not play out of doors: I can remember only two brothers whose house I went to, and no one ever coming to ours.)

There was only one occasion when I felt it really mattered to bring someone home. My classroom partner, the other half of the 'Prick'/'Wire' duo, now in the Sixth Form, had a sister who contracted chickenpox: the family doctor wanted him to live elsewhere until she ceased to be infectious. I put it to my mother that he should come to stay with us.

NO, was the answer.

I argued the case. As an act of charity. It would cause no trouble, no extra housework, no 'mess' . . . He was an intelligent, sensible youth, and I was sure she would like him. (I may say that our joint randiness never went beyond talk.) I really wanted him to stay with us.

NO.

I was dismayed – but not surprised, alas! I don't remember ever asking if I could bring anyone else to the house.

LVII

A curious thing has been happening in my memory. I have remarked that when I was young I saw my father through my mother's eyes, as a consequence of which it was not until many years later that I began to see him through my own eyes – and realised that he was a much nicer man than I had been thinking him to be. When I was young I saw my mother, whom I loved, through my own eyes – or was it, again, in some way through hers? Now, when I am writing about her in these pages, Memory has changed my vision to what I see through my own eyes of sixty years later . . . And that is different. I realise that *she* may have been a *less* nice woman than I thought she was.

That makes me feel sad. And yet, and yet . . . How little one knows of people, even one's mother and father. I have a clear remembrance of a man coming to the house one day, to the old house, and probably in Wartime – my father was not there. I can no longer remember in the least what he looked like, though I feel the impression he made on me was friendly. What I do remember exactly, absolutely exactly, is his name.

'This is Wilf Sadler.'

That's all.

The name cropped up very occasionally in my mother's later conversations, with no associated context; until a day – I must have been in my thirties – when my mother said:

'You know, Wilf Sadler wanted me to run away with him.'

'I didn't know,' I said, looking into her face with astonishment. I managed to add gently: 'Why didn't you?'

'He's the only man I ever would have run away with.'
She was thinking about him, not answering my question.
I repeated it.

'I stayed because of you children.'

There was nothing to say. Because of *me* . . .

She had said 'you children', meaning my sister as well;
which implied that he had still been trying to persuade her
at least two years after the War was over.

I was too inhibited to be able to carry on the conversation
any further, and so, I think, was she. That was the last I
heard of it. I have no idea if my father knew. Knowing her
secretiveness I should think almost certainly not.

And yet, and yet again . . . In old age she said to
me – and I cannot vouch for her being fully *compos* at
the time:

'You know, when I was a girl, I had lots of boyfriends.'
She paused, looking away from me. 'I think I married the
right one.' Another pause, then looking back again at me
with a sort of laugh – 'I *hope* I did!'

At this time I was in my sixties. And I was still
awed by how mysterious other people are.

LVIII

Reverting to earlier recollections of Ernie, and thoughts of
our growing apart . . . Each other's *alter ego* we might have
been in our pre-pubic days, yet I remember how different,
even then, were our ideas about what we wanted to be in
life. As a matter of fact I had no idea, myself: Ernie, his
ambition inflamed, I presume, by living for four years in
Crewe, singlemindedly fixed on becoming an engine-driver.

In Crewe we had only to lean over the nearest railway-bridge to see long heavy trains swirling at speed underneath us one after another; or make an excursion to the railway-station, where, standing on a platform, we could admire the huge locomotives within arm's reach – grandiose monsters of machinery, all the more overwhelming for their passionate bluster of steam. Glorious steam! (When years later I came across aristocrats who could claim they had been born with blue blood in their veins, I took to making a parallel proud claim that as a Crewe-boy I had been born with steam in mine.) Glorious steam – there was nothing like it!

London & North Western Railway locomotives were built in Crewe, giving the town a tremendous edge in prestige over Derby, where the carriages were made. Poor Derby! The locomotives were painted all black, with just some of their lines elegantly picked out in white and red: their only possible rivals were the locomotives of the Great Western Railway, which were painted a beautiful emerald green. (When the LNWR became the London Midland Scottish, some tasteless jack-in-office had all the grandiose black monsters changed to a dingy maroon.)

Ernie as a little boy longed to become an engine-driver. Yet it was I who had the experience, ten years later, that Ernie would have given his eyes for – I rode on the foot-plate of a locomotive. (A steam locomotive, of course.) The husband of my godmother, one of the four people ranged in front of me at my christening, was a minor boss in the railway company, and he arranged for my trip. He led me, negotiating a cat's cradle of railway lines, to the locomotive, and hoisted me up into the charge of the driver. It was a shunting-engine. I should have liked to ride on the footplate of the Royal Scot, but I supposed it would need Royalty to arrange that.

I was deeply impressed by the array of instruments facing the driver, the gauges with white enamel faces, the valves and levers, and what looked like a smallish driving-wheel polished to mirror-like brilliance; by the heat of the furnace with its red flicker coming under the door; and most of all by the piercing note of the steam-whistle as we chuff-chuff-*chuffed* into motion. And so we shunted up and down for half an hour. Throughout that time the driver not once, so far as I can recall, looked through the port-hole in his cabin; but leaned out at the side to read the signals.

Second thoughts on the instruments and controls. The driver knew where each one was, and explained its use to me; yet in my memory the array remains without any over-riding design, as if each new lever or gauge had been added, as it became necessary, in the nearest vacant space. I may be wrong.

Although Ernie's great ambition ten years later was not to be an engine-driver, I felt that somehow it would not be fair to tell him I'd had the thrilling experience of a ride on the footplate, even of a shunting-engine.

LIX

I remember, too, Liverpool from the other side of the river. Auntie Ede had gone to live there after the War, when her husband, an engineer, had got a job in Garston Docks. My father's youngest sister, with her easy-going, active, 'good sort' ways, she frequently invited me to stay during the holidays. By then she was very happy with having a healthy little son. Unfortunately he was too young to be company for me; so my uncle, who was a superintendent of some sort at the docks, found me interesting things to see there. Apart from that, my aunt would sometimes leave her 'girl' in charge of the little boy for the day, so that she could take me into Liverpool, a great metropolitan centre of attraction. Occasionally Ernie came over for a day from the other side of the river. And very occasionally my mother came for the day from Crewe. (With Crewe at the junction of the North Western Railway system, the local metropolitan centres of attraction, Liverpool, Manchester, Hanley, Chester, were little more than an hour's express train-ride away, sometimes no more than half an hour's.)

When my mother came we met her at Lime Street Station, and Auntie Ede conducted us round the metropolitan shops, especially those in a street which she regarded as the acme of superior taste. Since she had come to Garston her social aspirations were blossoming – most noticeably in a slightly haw-haw tone of refinement beginning to infuse her native speech. (In Garston she held afternoon bridge-parties for the wives of her husband's classier colleagues.) The acme was called Bold Street, and we sauntered up one side and down the other, looking into the shops. I didn't dis-enjoy it, but I should have been much happier mooching about with Ernie down on the landing-stage. Sadly, instead of remembering the names of the superior shops in Bold Street, I remember the names of the big less superior shops around the bottom end of it: the department stores were at the beginning of their rise to monopoly, the Bon Marché, Lewis's and, most memorable for me for the comical overblown Welshness of its name, Owen Owen's. My recollection of them is that they were much livelier and noisier than the shops of Bold Street, which gave an impression of calm and quiet, and, I suppose, of expensiveness. (Perhaps calm and quiet and expensiveness in shops go together.)

After a mid-day meal we sometimes went, all three of us, to the Walker Art Gallery, where I loved seeing famous pictures in the original, real paintings. At home our walls were decorated with a varied assortment of pictures. My father had a taste for etchings, and there were some quite pleasing specimens, chiefly pictures of old-fashioned towns – I think that if he had ever taken up his talent for drawing, he would have liked to make etchings himself. But among our modest collection of pictures, the one I liked above all was an oil-painting by the artist friend of Mary Elizabeth's who gave us the stencil-papers – gleaming yellow daffodils in a glass vase shaped like a goldfish bowl: the flowers looked touchingly like fresh daffodils and the artist had exactly caught the curved appearance of the stems due to refraction by the water. (Flo West: her name has suddenly come back to me.) For years I persuaded my mother not to dispose of the painting. On the other hand the picture which *provoked* me was the black-and-white photographic reproduction of a masterpiece that showed a woman, blind-fold, precariously sitting on top of a large ball, presumably meant to represent the earth. It was entitled *Hope*. I couldn't imagine what she might be hoping for – unless it were the stability of equilibrium necessary to prevent her slipping off the ball before the artist had time to finish painting her.

Sometimes when I was staying with her, Auntie Ede, possibly with an instinct for liberating me, sent me to the Walker Gallery for the afternoon on my own, while she and my mother went on a second circuit of the shops. Thus I developed a taste for solitary visits to Art Galleries. But when I was staying with Auntie Ede there were more exciting things to do, crowned for excitement by visits to the docks at Garston, where my uncle arranged for me two special excursions.

The first excursion was to watch banana-boats being unloaded. It was in the early days of mechanisation. The bunches of bananas from the ships' holds were thrown into loops formed by a moving canvas band passing downwards over a series of rollers on a structure beside the ship: at the bottom they were automatically ejected from the moving bands into crates. It now sounds simple enough, but it fascinated me then. Furthermore there was the frightening bonus of a banana bunch in one of the loops possibly housing a venomous Jamaican snake or a poisonous Jamaican spider . . .

The other excursion was out into the open sea in a dredger. The dredgers filled up their holds with sludge in the area of the docks, and then trudged out to discharge their cargo beyond the mouth of the Mersey. I was allowed by the captain to stand on the bridge so as not to miss anything. On the outward journey I paid due attention to the landmarks on the coast: the New Brighton Tower, of course, on one side; on the other side, Bootle; the famous golf-course of Ainsdale; Southport with its pier stretching for miles because the tide never came in . . . All very well on the outward journey, when the heavy ballast of sludge had a stabilising effect; but when the cargo had been discharged, the now lightened boat turned round to go back, and all was not necessarily very well, especially if we had struck a day of high wind and driving rain. I don't remember being sea-sick, but there were times when every ounce of a true Briton's Old Sea-Doggishness was called for. My uncle would be waiting for me on the quayside, clearly prepared to carry me ashore if necessary. There's a true delight in the self-congratulation which follows coming ashore from a rough passage without having been sick. And my uncle congratulated me, too.

LX

It was during this latter summer that the results of my School Certificate Examination came out, with the tally of Distinctions and Credits that I have recorded at the end of my account of my first years at CCSS. The die had been cast, the choice between taking the High Road and taking the Low Road; the choice between doing Arts or Science in the Sixth Form. I don't remember any of the masters at the school giving us advice individually, in fact I'm sure they didn't. The advice on which I acted came from my father.

The actual results in the different subjects for the examination did not give us – my father and I – a definite lead. I had shown myself to be equally good, or bad, at both Arts and Science. If I were more drawn to one than to the other, it was to Science. I can't say that at the age of not yet fifteen I was more inclined to thought that could be tested by referring it to observable reality, in the end by physical experiment, though that has turned out to be a lasting inclination in my nature. Perhaps it comes with the genes . . . Anyway I realise now that it was profoundly there, though it was not yet manifest to me or anyone else. At the time when we were making the decision I was acquiring some scientific hobbies: I was still interested in photography to some lesser extent, increasingly interested in wireless – I had embarked on building wireless-sets of my own. And I knew that I loved doing experiments in the school laboratories, even though some of those experiments were disappointing to me in that they did not seem to lead anywhere. No matter.

The impulse towards my decision came from my father.

The mid-1920s; troubles in society – many men already out of work and the prospect of more . . . My father happened to be the local secretary of the National Union of Teachers, which stimulated his foresight. I don't think the word 'slump' had yet made a prominent appearance in the jargon of the time, but the concept was in the offing. My father knew what it was about. I remember exactly what he said to me about my choice of career.

'A boy who's got a degree in science will never be short of a job.'

We were imagining what life would be like in the 1930s, what life would be like for the sort of industrial society in which we were currently embedded – the life of Crewe.

I don't remember what I said to him, but the die was in effect cast. The Science Sixth Form was my choice.

How right my father turned out to be!

LXI

Mathematics, Physics and Chemistry were called the Main subjects, and were compulsory. (The school didn't teach any Biology.) But there was a choice in what was called the Subsidiary subject. What a choice! Between English and French. English – more of *Bodge*! That was the end of that. Thus it was that I terminated my formal education in English Literature at the age of fourteen.

I had already enjoyed learning French. I now saw the prospect that later on I might go over to France and be able to converse with people who lived there. How much headway I thought I was going to make in two or three years of two lessons a week, I don't know. On the other hand I *can* say that when I do go over there I sometimes hear myself using the subjunctive mood correctly!

LXII

As a treat, that summer, my father took me to London to see the Wembley Exhibition. I had never set foot in London before, and I was enthralled by the national pavilions – I took photographs galore. The photograph which took my fancy above the rest, the record I most treasured, was that of the domed gateway to the Indian pavilion. My first sight of the architecture of the Orient. I never forgot it. But architecture of the Orient, indeed! When decades later I went to India I realised when I reached New Delhi that my schoolboy fancy had been taken by an example of architecture not Indian Indian but *Lutyens* Indian – heavy and flat compared with the lightness and grace of the real thing. Yet I can still see that old sepia photograph, epitomising an Indian gateway . . .

LXIII

A month or so later I entered the Science Sixth Form at CCSS – it included *two girls*!

Up to the Fifth Form boys and girls were taught separately. They were brought together full-time in the Sixth: but in the past girls had always gone into the Arts Sixth, never, so far as we knew, into the Science Sixth

– Science was 'not a girls' subject'. So our two girls were able to congratulate themselves on being pioneers, while we regarded their presence as a miraculous bonus. They found the warmest of welcomes in seven or eight boys, from whom they could select at will two or three companions with whom to perambulate the playing-field whenever they felt like it. So far as I can recall, this didn't stir intense sexual rivalry among us: the pleasure of their company arose simply from the fact that – I don't quite know how to put it . . . the fact that they were females of the species and we were males? As if metaphorically-speaking the two had different smells that were alluring to each other – that over-played basis for advertising scent? (Speaking non-metaphorically I can say that, those being the days before deodorants, girls actually did have different smells, quite noticeable at dances; as I suppose we boys did, too. While among the classrooms, for instance, girls' classrooms always smelt faintly of onions . . .)

Our girls were an agreeable pair, neither of them staggeringly beautiful – in fact, looking back on it now, one might say there was from that point of view nothing to choose between them. And from a personal point of view they were equally likeable. One was a substantial girl with shining rosy cheeks and brown button-eyes: she had dark curly hair which hung in corkscrews. Daughter of a grocer who owned a flourishing shop in a street not far from where my paternal grandfather, painter and decorator, lived. The other girl was taller, slender, with fair hair 'shingled' (a fashion of the time), and a rather beaky nose. Daughter of a milliner with a flourishing hat-shop on the main road near the railway-station. (My mother occasionally bought a hat there.)

In Crewe a milliner's social cachet was higher than

a grocer's, but that was not the reason for my finding something to choose between them. The milliner's
daughter wore a very short gym-tunic, hitched up high
with the black and orange CCSS cord round her hips,
thus displaying navy-blue knickers and long shapely legs –
which brought me face to face with what actually there was
to choose between them. (The other girl habitually wore a
skirt.) The highest gym-tunic in the school . . . She was
the one I pursued to be my partner at school dances, as an
alternative to the carmine-cheeked poetess in the making. I
felt a sharp discouragement when I heard that she already
had a boy, not at the school. (By the way, in those days we
talked about a girl having a 'boy' or a boy having a 'girl':
the rather arch-sounding 'boy-friend' and 'girl-friend' had
not yet come in.)

The company of the two girls was something new for
us, attractive in itself. There was no regular pairing off –
in class they sat together, at playtime we perambulated the
playing-field with them at their choice. Perambulating the
playing-field – the thought suddenly evokes a sharp visual
image of us. I have described how the girls were dressed:
I suddenly see the boys' mode of the times. We wore suits,
or blazers and flannels, shirts with collars, and school ties.
In the Sixth Form several of us, I was one, wore a black
jacket and pin-striped trousers: in hot weather we shed
the tie and wore the shirt-collar outside the jacket. What
strikes me as odd is the fashion, when perambulating, for
wearing the jacket buttoned up and thrusting our hands in
our trouser pockets by pushing back the front flaps of the
jacket: though it revealed the trouser-flies it was quite free
from any element – and I have to say this in view of the later
appearance of Levis – of masculine display. Innocent.

So life in the Sixth Form settled down pleasantly. With

only so few of us in the labs, there was scope for more interesting experiments which, if they didn't necessarily seem to
be leading very far, did – in comparison with the random
collection of little experiments we had done earlier – give
us the impression of leading *somewhere*. We were allowed
to use the more sensitive balances for weighing things. We
were taught to make notes. It was the beginning of science
as a serious study, rather than an adjunct to a bunch of
miscellaneous subjects, though I was not powerfully aware
of this at the time. An odd recollection: in the second-year
Practical Chemistry, we were given every Friday afternoon a
mixture of chemical substances and told to discover – using
a book setting out tables of analytical procedure – what the
components were. That was really exciting!

LXIV

In the meantime my musical studies were advancing at home
after school, not to mention at home illicitly during school
hours; a lot of my time spent on practising 'pieces', too little
of my time spent on practising 'scales and arpeggios'. I can
remember being asked at one lesson to play scales that I
hadn't touched since the previous lesson – regrettably. It
occurs to me that when I observe that I liked to learn things,
I have to qualify that by specifying that they were those
things which seemed to me to *say* something. (At a further
remove Multiplication Tables, for instance, said something
about numbers, as well as being of practical use.) Only too
late did I realise that scales and arpeggios said something
about the musical effect of differently-constructed series of
notes – obviously skill in playing them was of great use in

enabling one to nip up and down the keyboard at speed. With deplorable absence of foresight I was willing to do my duty by Czerny's exercises and Wieck's only for the purpose of despatching them in order to get on to the 'pieces'.

So I arrive at trying to remember what on earth the pieces were. Next-door to impossible. The first I recall – accurately! – was 'To a Wild Rose' by MacDowell; then something about a water-lily or a swan by a Finn called Palmgren. From them I somehow got to early sonatas by Beethoven. Then Bach's Two-Part Inventions – at the time the Three-Part were thought to be too difficult. In due course I came to selected Chopin Studies, which gave me great pleasure. (I'm not sure if it was then that I discovered the hyper-romantic effect to be achieved by playing one hand in advance of the other – immediately put down by my teacher. 'What *do* you think you're doing, Harry? Artur Rubinstein always plays both hands together. So should you!') Then there was what seems to me now a 'sport', for covering the keyboard at speed, a piece called 'Etincelles' by Moskowski (which I heard to my stupefaction played at a recital in the 1980s – something by Horowitz!) Now – bringing me towards the time when I was going to leave CCSS – Schumann's 'Davidsbündler', and by Brahms a 'Rhapsody' and the 'Capriccio on a Theme by Paganini'. Liszt's 'Waldesrauschen' came into the story somewhere; and – representing contemporary music – a piece by Arnold Bax. I was about to say no Debussy, but I'm pretty sure that 'Clair de Lune' crept in, and possibly an 'Arabesque'.

I feel I've made a very poor job of remembering my list of solo pieces. This doesn't matter to me, but I'm afraid I'm doing a regrettable disservice to an excellent teacher.

In addition to the solo pieces there were at home two symphonies arranged as piano duets for four hands,

Beethoven's Fifth and a symphony by Mozart whose key and Köchel number I don't recall. It was my mother and father who had bought the duets, and in due course it was my hands which became two of the four, the other two being my mother's or more often my father's. I played the top part, my father the bottom; with my mother, the other way round. It was an exhilarating experience, with all our wrong notes which there was no opening to correct. (I had a habit of exasperating my mother, when I was practising alone, of going back, whenever I played a wrong note, and getting it right.)

Actually Beethoven's Fifth as a duet was used by my music-teacher, having inducted me into analysis of sonata form via the sonatas I played, to launch me on the more daunting task of trying to find a way through symphonic form. I was interested, and my teacher was pleased with my efforts. Not that her pleasure in my efforts was universal. Truthfulness compels me to add that, at so to speak the opposite extreme from sonata-form analysis, she was never universally pleased, when it came to my sitting down and playing the piano, with my *rubato* –

'It's as if you keep it in a bottle,' she said to me one day, 'and pour a bit out when you think you should.'

However, in spite of my fallings-short as performer, my music-teacher asked me to take part in a small public concert she was organising for her pupils. I was about sixteen at the time. The star pupil of the concert was a girl, about the same age as me – I'll call her K.H. – who played piano solos: I played duos with a rising young local cellist who subsequently became a professional musician. I don't remember who else, if anyone, played. I remember only K.H. The concert took place in the hall of a nearby school – not CCSS, with which my teacher was too grand

111

to have any connection. I can still call up the frightening and exhilarating sensations of my first appearance on a public platform – and still call up the tender and stirring emotions of being there in the presence of K.H. I was in the first throes of romantic love.

K's weekly music-lesson followed immediately after mine, and she would come straight up to the music-room, carrying her satchel, while I was gathering together my belongings ready for leaving. At the doorway, in the shaded light which came from the lamp focused on the piano, she looked more beautiful, more mysteriously beautiful, than any other girl I had ever seen. The sparkle of her eyes penetrated the distance between us; the sheen of her hair – it was cut just below the nape of her neck – shifted kaleidoscopically as she crossed the room. (In daylight her eyes were blue as the sea, her complexion clear as a summer's dawn – to me.) Seeing her I yearned for her as a boy yearns for a star – only too appropriately, as I thought she was miles above me in the social scale.

In greeting K. and saying goodbye to me, our teacher joined us for a few moments in three-cornered conversation. So innocent was I at the time that it didn't occur to me that our teacher might sentimentally be bringing together two of her favourite pupils, K. her first favourite, I perhaps her second. These moments of conversation sank into my soul. When I left the house I loitered on the pavement outside for a few minutes, trying to listen to K. playing; and then I walked the neighbouring streets in an uplifted state for one hour minus those few minutes, so as to arrive back, if I were lucky, just in time to run into her – accidentally, of course – when she was leaving. I was not lucky. I never knew if she sometimes left earlier, or if our teacher kept her for a longer spell. But unluckiest of all was when I got back just at the right time, to see a car roll up to the pavement – her brother, come to take her home.

She lived in Nantwich. Crewe, an ugly little urban product of the Industrial Revolution, was built for the working-classes. Nantwich was a pretty little country town, with a quiet atmosphere and black-and-white buildings which survived from the seventeenth century; in some of the houses around lived well-off bourgeois people. From our teacher and from K.H.'s own appearance and manner I had picked up the idea that her family were pretty well-off: I don't remember what they were – cheese-factors or something. Actually her surname was well known in the Cheshire countryside: I realised that I'd heard it in the conversation of my mother's maternal relations who lived there. Good Wesleyans all, they were.

The concert, with rehearsals as well as performance, gave me the opportunity to see K. and talk to her for much longer than ever before, to talk to her when our teacher was occupied with something else. Though she was miles above me, like a star, we got on quite well. I tried to interest her, and watched her face begin faintly to glow. She had a short straight nose and a pretty chin. After the concert, when we were both faintly glowing – it had been a success: she had played beautifully and I hadn't disgraced myself – I plucked up courage to ask her if I could take her to a CCSS school-dance. She said Yes!

LXV

It was the dance at which the school regularly celebrated the ending of a summer term. The Hall was emptied of furniture excepting the platform, on which a small amateur dance-band was installed, and a single row of chairs against the walls. The polished parquet floor had been sprinkled with french chalk to make it more slippery for dancing. Hanging from the ceiling were softly-coloured Japanese lanterns; in the centre a revolving globe with bits of looking-glass stuck to it, reflecting shafts of light. A romantic setting!

I waited for her inside the front entrance to the school, the entrance for visitors – pupils entered by the two side-entrances. I was wearing a new suit, a formal suit which I was to wear out by daily use in the Sixth Form. Black jacket and grey striped trousers – several of the other boys in the Sixth Form had similar outfits. Mine had been made for me by a little tailor in the Nantwich Road, Bobby Moseley. All my suits were made for me: I remember the advent of Burton's and suchlike vendors of ready-made suits many, many years later. (I don't know who made the working-men's suits that Mary Elizabeth's customers brought in to pawn.) I was satisfied that the suit fitted me, and I was confident in the dancing-lessons that my mother had been sending me to for the last year. I was waiting for K.H. Would she come?

A sudden thought. 'I don't *know* her, not really . . . '

Behind me, in the Hall, the little band began to play.

The front door of the entrance hall swung open, and there she was – accompanied by her brother. She was wearing a dark top-coat over a dance-dress that was made of rustling tissue-paper-like silk, radiantly the colour of apricots. Her brother courteously handed her over to me; he was older and taller than me, and his accent was superior to mine. He enquired when the dance was due to end, and then arranged to come back for her. My spirits fell; the most romantic peak of the school-dance, way beyond the peaks of taking one's partner in to supper and dancing the last waltz with her, was not to be mine – walking her home. Her brother had a car.

I busied myself with showing her the way to the cloak-room, and then lined up with the other boys waiting for their girls to come out. The band was playing, a few couples were already dancing. I felt too nervous to speak.

When she did come out I managed to smile. 'Shall we dance straight away? May I have the pleasure?' (The dancing-lesson formula.)

'Oh, yes.'

So we danced. She danced quite well: I was much too shy to tell her so, but something came into the atmosphere, relaxation, relief, pleasure . . . We were over the first hurdle. If necessary we could stay on the dance-floor all evening, dancing together.

The dance ended and we had to move off the floor and find somewhere to sit down. I launched into explanations – there would be some supper, at about half-past nine, in one of the classrooms over there. 'Are you hungry?'

She laughed at me. 'Not yet.' She went on laughing. 'Are you?'

'Not yet,' I said.

Silence. We glanced round the room, at the other boys and girls. Among them I saw the poetess in the making, narrow brown eyes and carmine cheeks – she was wearing a carmine dress. How different it was to be out with *her*!

115

I looked at K. a little pale perhaps, yet smiling and in charge of the situation. Like a star, way above me, now for the moment down to earth in a chair beside me. I had yearned for her: here she was. I had got what I had dreamed about. Simultaneously I had distant intimations of getting what I had asked for – somewhere over the horizon there was something telling me about dreams that come true having to be coped with.

The band started up again.

'May I have the pleasure?' I said decisively.

This time on the floor we began to talk to each other. Dancing together was easy and conversation was possible. My spirits began to rise. As we chatted and smiled at each other, I noticed other couples looking at us. I had a beautiful girl in my arms.

We began talking about our music-lessons, of course, and about out music-teacher.

'Did she tell *you* all the things you did wrong at the concert?' K. asked.

'Well, not really . . . ' I was so astonished by the idea of K. not being above criticism that for the moment I couldn't remember any criticism of myself.

When we sat down again K. enumerated the criticisms of herself. She didn't seem to realise, or to care, that she was reducing the distance between herself and me. I had double feelings. She was alas! less of the star way above me, subject of my ethereal longings; yet more within my down-to-earth reach, someone I could be in love with to more purpose. I began to look at her with less yearning and more specific attraction. My spirits rose again. This was going to be a wonderful evening.

We danced on, and in between times talked on. There was music to be talked about, 'Are you going to become a musician?' I asked. 'A pianist? You know, a concert-pianist?'

'Oh no.' Her tone of voice was gentle yet dismissive.

'What a pity! You're so good.'

'Are you?' She was smiling at me. 'Are you going to?'

Somehow her teasing – and I felt it was teasing – deflated me. It had dismissed the idea for *me*. I was not as good as she was, I knew. But . . .

'Why are you *not*?' I said. 'I mean, why aren't you going to go in for music as a career?'

'I don't think it would be quite right. Not for me. You know . . . ' She stretched back a little so as to look into my face. 'Would it be right for you?' She was smiling at me, laughing at me . . .

, 'I don't know.' I did know at that moment: she had somehow taken away some of my desire to go in for music. Only for that moment? Perhaps the desire would come back when she had gone.

'What *are* you going to do?' I said. 'Are you going to go on with music-lessons?'

She laughed a pleasing laugh. 'Oh yes, for ever, I expect!'

For a little while we then talked about our families. I noticed how sweetly she pronounced 'My mother and my father', when I blunderingly said 'Me muther and me fa-ather'. (I was schooling myself not to say 'Aye' all the time in place of 'Yes'.) Her parents lived in a style quite different to mine. The future she foresaw for herself seemed to consist mainly of shopping expeditions with her mother to Chester, and tennis-parties at the houses of families living round about. When she was not doing her music-practice, of course.

Money, class . . . All so different from the style in which I was immersed. So *superior*.

'What are you looking forward to, most of all?' I asked. 'In the future.'

Instantly she laughed. 'I want a car of my own!'

'I do hope you get one.' For a moment I was visited by an idiotic fantasy of her driving me out in it. A different way of life. A life with *her*.

'This *is* a nice dance,' she said.

Her eyes, blue as the sea, had acquired a sparkle that I hadn't seen before. Her exquisite-complexioned cheeks, previously pale, seemed to be catching a reflected glow from the apricot colour of her dress – the colour made her hair look darker. Dancing again she didn't press her body against mine, yet she didn't hold herself apart. We were coming up to the supper-interval.

I managed to find a table for two – most were for four, and I didn't want to join one of the other boys and his partner. That, I began to realise, was a mistake; for although I occupied myself with carrying sandwiches and trifle and lemonade to and fro, our conversation in the supper-room seemed to be wilting. It would have helped to have had company to keep things going. At a nearby table I saw the carmine-cheeked one giving me an exploratory look: *her* partner was the tall, mature-looking youth who went for extra tuition to the schoolmistress who lived across the road from us. Though I had the most beautiful girl in the room as *my* partner and I was head over heels in love with her, I was – just for a moment – jealous of that youth.

When we were leaving the supper-room another boy whom I knew came within such close range that I had to introduce him to K., reluctantly; when he looked as if he were going to ask her for a dance, discouragingly. This, while knowing that K. and I had reached the stage of the evening when we both needed a change of partner.

With the supper-interval over, we settled down again to the dance.

'Ladies and Gentlemen,' called the MC, 'the next dance will be an Excuse-Me!'

There was a buzz of approval round the room. An opportunity to take away another boy's partner, to have a change! The band struck up. Looking round for a sight of the carmine dress, I rose to my feet. To realise that K. was still sitting down.

'I don't think I'll dance this one, Harry.'

I had to sit down again. I didn't feel that she was governed so much by intention to stick to me as by intention not to let herself be available to any of those other boys on the floor. (It didn't occur to me that she didn't know any of them.)

I argued that we could go on the floor and not permit an Excuse-Me. She smiled.

'I don't think that would be fair.' Firm – and setting a distance between us.

Yet when the the next dance was announced she stood up in front of me before I could say 'May I have the pleasure?' I can see her now, her face shining with high spirits. We danced again.

And when it came to the last waltz I felt she was almost leaning against me. I was carried away by the joy of the moment.

All the lights were switched off in the Japanese lanterns, and the darkness was pierced only at random by the reflected shafts of light from the globe revolving above our heads, the globe with its surface sprinkled with mirrors, the shafts of light turning.

It was usual, while this was going on, surreptitiously to kiss one's partner as one whirled round in the waltz.

I glanced at K. We were just passing a boy who clearly was surreptitiously kissing his partner. K. glanced at me in the darkness. She was smiling still, and leaning against me. Surreptitiously I kissed her, just below the temple. I was in heaven.

And what did *she* do? She appeared not to notice. For days afterwards I tried to make up my mind about it – had she noticed my kissing her or had she not? As we went past the main doorway to the entrance hall, she said quietly:

'There's my brother.'

He had come to take her home.

The waltz came to an end. I took her across to the cloakroom, waited for her, and escorted her back to her brother. He was courteous to me, but distant, very distant.

'Thank you, Harry.' She held out her hand to me. I took it. 'I've enjoyed it terribly.'

I tightened my hold on her fingers – and I think she did the same to mine.

Around me I heard other boys saying, 'Ta-ra, Nancy!' and 'Ta-ra, Madge!' to girls whose fathers had come to fetch them home.

I said 'Goodbye!' to K.

How long was it Goodbye for? Somehow the excitement was fading. Even under the influence of what remained of it, something was telling me, 'You can't really keep this going . . . '

A few minutes later I was outside the school, on the pavement, in the night. Around me now were other boys privileged to walk their partners home. Some of them, whose partners lived well outside the town, had a trudge of several miles ahead of them. *I* had only fifty yards to go.

LXVI

My first appearance on the concert-platform, and my relative success there, provoked an astonishing response in my father. A few days later he said:

'Do you want to change your mind, and go in for music? Because if you do, we're prepared to let you go to a conservatoire. In Paris. Or Moscow.'

I had no idea that he and my mother had been discussing it in such terms, that he and my mother knew anything about conservatoires in Paris or Moscow. I knew nothing myself, apart from the fact that they existed. I couldn't believe my parents knew more. Yet with the utmost generosity they had made me the offer.

I was momentarily overwhelmed with gratitude and excitement. The thought of studying in Paris or Moscow was amazing. I let my imagination loose on it.

'Think about it, lad!'

'I will!'

Overwhelmed and excited I imagined the prospect as if it were possible.

I had no doubt that my father would make all the necessary enquiries, and subsequently take all the necessary steps, including finding the money (though I didn't know how). Where the prospect failed was on my side, in me. To get into a foreign conservatoire, or even the Royal College of Music, one would have to show evidence of studies and performance incalculably beyond anything I had to offer. I didn't know how far one's studies and performance would have to have gone, but now, confronted with the question directly, I did know my own couldn't have. I had never thought of discussing it with my music-teacher. (I imagined one would probably have had to be able to sit down at the piano and play a Mozart sonata from memory at the age of six.)

And if by some miracle I were able to get a scholarship for studying in one of these cities, what was I to make of it when I came out? I knew by now that I simply had to escape from Crewe; but willy-nilly my horizons were still Crewe horizons – where was I to get any other horizons from? I didn't possess the dazzling talent at the keyboard which would ultimately ensure me invitations to perform at Celebrity Concerts. (I had just been taken to one or two of such concerts at Hanley.) I was completely ignorant of any scope to compose: I had never even thought of such a thing, of any living person composing. I saw myself ending up like my own music-teacher – she had studied 'abroad' – whom I admired so much, spending my days on giving hourly lessons to children from the streets of towns like Crewe, if not Crewe itself.

I promised my father to think about going to a conservatoire. I did think about it. I imagined myself in Moscow with the streets under snow and sleighs jingling by. I imagined myself at student cafés in Paris, drinking cup after cup of black coffee, and – who knows? – perhaps a glass of absinthe. (At this time I had never set foot outside England.) I imagined; while all the time somehow knowing *au fond* that there was practically no connection between these imaginings and reality.

Yet in writing this I am not being completely honest, that is to say I was not questioning my parents' marvellously generous offer sheerly because it was obstructed by technical difficulties, let alone being possibly on the cards in the first place. I was not turning it down and leaving a vacuum in the future.

I had another idea – previously called my unheard-of intention! – so unheard-of that up to now I had kept it entirely to myself.

LXVII

It is obvious to me now, and must be obvious, I'm sure, to anyone reading this, that my talent for music in the first place and my capacity for giving my mind to it in the second, were such that I could *never* have made a professional career of it. My parents and I had been prepared to discuss my doing so in the light of our experience of Crewe: by the light of the world in general it was totally unrealistic.

LXVIII

Ever since I was fourteen – until the present, as a matter of fact – I have looked back with incomprehension upon how and why the idea first crossed my mind. I had taken it into my head that I wanted to go to Cambridge University, of all places.

No other university would do. It was to be Cambridge. I knew nothing about Cambridge University, apart from its being *the* place for science. I knew nobody who had been there: no boy from the school had ever gone to Cambridge – or Oxford, either. Everyone at CCSS, boys and girls, went to Manchester University or Liverpool University, or just possibly to one of the colleges of London University. For a boy at CCSS to think of going to Cambridge was unheard-of – that's why I had taken care that nobody at CCSS should hear of it.

It was only when I realised that I was sheering away from the offer of studying music abroad, whether I were capable of it or not, that I felt I simply had to let my father and mother into the secret of an ambition that I had been concealing for a couple of years at least. I told them.

My mother and father said *they* would think about it.

My secret was out, and I felt strangely relieved, not merely in a superficial sense. Somehow the fact of its being out made me feel with inner conviction that the day might really come when I would go to Cambridge.

LXIX

Working for my Higher School Certificate. When I went into the Sixth Form the sleeping arrangements in our house had been changed around so as to give me a separate room in which to work. I was agreeable to it. I had given up my little bedroom overlooking the fields and the allotments, had given it up to my sister, now old enough to have a room away from everyone else at the back of the house. I had moved into the middle bedroom, while the so-called boxroom was converted for me into a suitable working-place by the introduction of a large desk with an American-leather-covered top supported by two pillars on each side composed of drawers. Unfortunately the window looked out into a comparable window, a few yards away, of the house next door; so the lower panes, instead of being transparent, were made of frosted glass, its opacity created by an irregular spiky pattern which looked like the crystals of ice that are formed from the moisture on panes of plain glass during frosty weather. The upper half looked over a roof. Nothing to distract me from my work.

Solitary up in that room I spent hours between properly working-and-reading and sinfully day-dreaming. My parents, dissatisfied with the teaching at CCSS enrolled me during the second year in a correspondence course, so that as well as school homework I had questions from a tutor to answer in soft blue-backed notebooks that were duly posted off – and came posted back with comments that I didn't always show my parents.

The room was quiet and warm. In winter it was heated by an oil-stove, a rather handsome object made of cast-iron, a hefty square-sectioned pillar with small curved feet and a handsome lid curved up to a finial, the feet and the lid being lacily perforated. When the stove was lit the light from the two lines of wick shone through a red glass window in the side of the pillar and projected through the lid a bright lacy pattern on the ceiling above. Incidentally I went on calling the room the boxroom – the 'study' didn't sound at all right for me, even if it marked a stage in my pursuit of the ambitious romantic dream of going to Cambridge.

I remember that it was while I was reading something – I don't remember what – up in the boxroom one night, a word suddenly stood out unforgettably from the page. Now an adolescent youth I was struck by this word exactly as I was struck when I was a little boy by the word 'abduct'. I was hideously struck by it. The word was 'self-abuse'. Until this moment the subject had been one for lewd schoolboy-joking. One went up to another boy in the playground and said:

'You know it makes hairs grow in the palm of your hand?'

And then waited for him to take his hand out of his pocket and look.

In the same vein, my surname minus the letter H offered other boys an irresistible temptation to change my Christian name to Thos.

Now all was changed. 'Self-abuse'. Why is it that giving a word to something invariably transforms it, usually into something awful? ('God' provides a most striking case in point.) The word sank into my imagination, causing an upheaval that lasted for months. Would my health break down? Would I go mad and fail my Higher School Certificate examination?

In whom could I confide? From other boys I didn't expect any good advice. Among adults I knew only my mother and father. My father was *out*, just that. Which left my mother. I thought and thought about it, till finally, lost to reason, I decided to confide in her. I remember sitting in a lighted railway-carriage one night, coming home from a concert in Manchester, and framing what I was going to say to her next day. (The thought of what would have ensued makes my hair stand on end.) The next day came. And vestiges of common sense which underlay my hysteria rose to the surface and took command. I did *not* tell my mother. Or anyone else. What did I do? I suppose one might say I soldiered on . . .

My health remained as robust as ever. I did not go mad, at least I am unaware of having done so. And jumping ahead a little way in time, I can announce that I passed my Higher School Certificate examination with a certain degree of acclaim.

LXX

Commenting on my 'robust' health brings back a recollection of the one serious illness I had in my youth. It began with a 'chill' and was diagnosed by our doctor as colitis –

'It's like having pneumonia in your lower regions,' he told me; a remark which puzzled me then and still does.

Anyway it was serious, very serious, we were told. My temperature went up into the 100°s for days, and I remember my mother and father taking it in turns to come up to my bedroom and sponge my body with cool water in the hope of bringing my temperature down. (I have a visual recollection of steam – water vapour – rising from my body when they did it: I should think this is probably invented.)

Doctors and parents always look for causes of whatever happens to one. The cause of my chill was identified unerringly: I had gone swimming with a party of boys from school one very cold morning at the local swimming baths; and, instead of getting dressed immediately after coming out of the water, I had hung about for a long time beside the bath with my icy-cold, clammy, wet towel wrapped round my middle, shivering – no hot showers in those days at public baths! I had to own up . . .

So, to the point of my recording the episode. In late age I occasionally search in desperation for relief from arthritic pains by going to a Turkish bath. The convention at this particular bath is to spend one's time, from immediately after one's first shower, with a long thin towel, clammy and soaking, wrapped round one's middle. I find myself draping

127

the towel over my shoulder, carrying it on my arm, holding
in it my hand – anything, after sixty years, but wrapping it
round my 'lower regions' . . .

Over one's *nature* the genes reign supreme. Over one's
behaviour trivial meaningless incidents can have their way
for a lifetime.

LXXI

The 1920s – Marconi, wireless, the British Broadcasting
Company . . . I had signalised my accession to the Science
Sixth by embarking on a course of building more and more
satisfactory wireless-sets, first with one valve, then two,
and so on – I think I ended up with at least four, because
I'm pretty certain, in fact quite certain, that I finally built
what was called a superheterodyne receiver. (Helpful journals came on to the market, *Wireless World* and *Popular
Wireless*.)

I had begun with a crystal set. The crystal was a little multi-
faceted, shiny, greyish lump, held in a little brass cup, elec-
trical contact with the crystal's upper surface established by
the tip of a spiral of fine brass wire called the 'cat's whisker'.
The effectiveness of the device depended on finding, by trial
and error, the best place on the surface of the crystal for the
cat's whisker to touch it at. As the cat's whisker was delicate
and springy, it was only too easily disturbed by somebody
walking past it. A condenser, a coil, a battery – simplicity
itself – arranged on a small card-table, stationed well out of
everybody's way in the (rarely-used) dining-room, close to a
french window through the frame of which was threaded a
lead from the aerial which stretched from the roof to a tree

at the bottom of the garden. One listened with headphones. Music came through as a delicious, tinkling sound. (I remark upon this fact because general received opinion was that on changing from a crystal to thermionic valves the sound became less *pure* . ...)

I remember my first valve set very clearly. It was housed in a wooden box with a sloping front. (I must have bought the box, since I possessed neither the tools nor the innate skill for carpentry: though I enjoyed the carpentry classes in my first two years at CCSS, my dovetail joints always needed a more than invisible packing of sawdust.) The sloping front was a panel of black, matt-surfaced insulating material called ebonite. Standing out from the middle of it was a single thermionic valve; through the internal silvering of the glass one could see the filament glowing down the centre of the cylindrical electrodes. A dial for the rheostat, which controlled the current through the filament; a dial for the condenser which controlled the tuning; and sticking out from the side of the box two coils, one fixed, the other movable by means of a lever. Moving the second coil nearer to the first resulted in a build-up, by a phenomenon which I learnt to call 'feed-back', in the level of sound in the earphones; till a point was reached when the set swung over from receiving oscillations from the BBC to transmitting oscillations of its own accord – audible as a whistling, howling sound (commonly referred to simply as 'oscillating'). On a busy listening-in night the ether was filled with whistling howls from neighbouring sets near and far.

Obviously the point of building a wireless-set was to listen ('listen-in', as it was called) to the BBC's broadcasts; but the most exciting moment in the process of building was the moment of switching on for the very first time – to see if there was any sound coming out of it at all. On the reverse side of the panel the components were connected by wires which had to be soldered on to terminals. In the early days there were no neat little electric soldering-irons, and I had to teach myself to manipulate a full-sized iron heated at the gas-stove. (I can still remember the smell of hot 'fluxite'.) It was only too easy for a beginner to pass a 'dry-joint', i.e. an apparent soldering which in reality left a fine air-gap. Switching on for the first time – not a sound! A wiring check with the circuit diagram – all correct. Then the hunt for the dry-joint, the main instrument for the purpose being a wetted finger . . . But sometimes everything went well – what makes me quite certain that I built a 'super-het' is the recollection that 'lining it up', contrary to what the journals had led me to be prepared for, gave me no trouble at all – I simply couldn't believe my luck. It worked!

LXXII

I ask myself now what on earth I listened to. I know there was an announcer called Alvar Liddell whose voice, in beautifully articulated pronunciation, I could recognise for many years after he gave up regular announcing. I read that he wore evening-dress for his work, and I thought that was rather nice. (An incipient taste for elegance?) The family must have listened to real music. There were three pairs of headphones running from a little distribution point, headphones later on to be replaced by a loudspeaker, a swan-necked Amplion with horn composed of petal-shaped panels of wood. We must have listened to real music because I remember my father's aversion to

130

the music of Stravinsky: I don't think my mother cared over-much for Stravinsky, but my father's objection was passionately vocal – Stravinsky might have been the Devil Incarnate of Music.

I now have to record what music I listened to on my own. Carroll Gibbons and his Savoy Orpheans. I remember an actual piece they played – 'Whisp'ring'. (The second syllable had to be dropped to accommodate the tune.) The first line went 'Whisp'ring the while I hold you nea-rer . . . ' The cause of my remembering it so amazingly well is not the beauty of the tune nor the poetry of the words. It's the indelible imprint on my memory of a transmogrified version we chanted in the school playground –

> I'd like to sleep with Nazimo-va,
> I'd smack her bum and turn her o-ver . . .

How can one express anything but delight in the Selectivity of Memory?

Lastly, to complete my recollections of listening-in, I have to quote the most memorable of all words with which the boss of the British Broadcasting Company, one Captain P. P. Eckersley, invariably concluded his broadcasts to the nation. Down six decades they still echo in my ears. To all listeners –

'DON'T OSCILLATE!' (Pause.) 'DON'T OSCILLATE!'

LXXIII

I took to going out regularly to see my mother's maternal relations in the country.

My mother went rarely, taking me with her, when I was little. I think the countryside reminded her too strongly of what she had suffered there during her childhood. Though the people were kindly enough now, her emotions towards them seemed to be permanently curdled, though she didn't say so, by resentment. I was subject to no such complications. I struck up a friendship with one of my cousins, a youth almost the same age as myself.

From the visits with my mother when I was little I can remember the Coopers, her maternal grandfather, formerly the village blacksmith, and her maternal grandmother. They were both in their nineties, the old man lean and stooping, the old woman small and birdlike. They were both near-blind from cataracts – for which there was then, for the likes of them, being poor and remotely situated, no treatment. I remember them creeping round their little house by touching the walls and the pieces of furniture.

Their son, my mother's uncle, who followed as village blacksmith, was at that time still alive, a short powerful fellow – he died early of sleeping sickness, which was in those days nearly always fatal. I remember watching him at work in the smithy; seeing golden sparks shower from the slices of red-hot iron as he hammered them into horseshoes, hearing the menacing hiss when he plunged them into cold water to temper them, smelling the burnt cuticle while he nailed them on to the hooves of the horses,

the unprotesting horses. Corny though it may sound I was
moved by admiration. Physical strength and natural intelligence; doing a service for his neighbours, and their animals
as well . . . If blacksmith's blood has come down through
three generations from his father to me, I'm glad of it. (Alas!
my mother's only story about him – typical and regrettable
– was a recollection of his coming across her, when she was
a little girl, weeing beside a ditch, and of his pushing her
backwards and bare-bottomed into a bed of nettles.)

After his death his widow went on living in the same
house with their daughter and two sons. In my recollection it
seems a gloomy old house, possibly because the ceilings were
low and big trees surrounding it kept out the light: I think
the place must once have been a farm of sorts, the house a
farmhouse. In these latter days there were chickens running
about the yard and a cow in the field. Among the outhouses
were stables, now unused, and barns; and an outside privy of
the type known as a 'two-holer'. (Though I don't recall its
ever being used by two persons simultaneously, I viewed it
with astonishment nevertheless.)

I struck up a friendship with the younger son, my
mother's cousin – technically my first cousin once removed.
I teased him, on the grounds of my being a later generation
than his, by calling him 'Uncle'. It was specially amusing – to
me – to have an uncle younger than myself. I liked him very
much. Short, broad-shouldered, physically strong, he was a
champion cross-country runner. (The latter accomplishment
could be to my disadvantage. After launching at him some
schoolboy insult, I would promptly take to my heels – I was
moderately quick off the mark. He didn't hurry himself in
pursuit: the moment came when my breath began to run
out and I heard the same steady plod, plod, plod coming
on behind me . . .)

I used to cycle out on summer evenings. I forget how long it took me – three-quarters of an hour, perhaps. From his house we went to pick up two of his friends; the three of them, intelligent lively youths, went to the same school – Sandbach Grammar School, classier than CCSS! The four of us then set out to roam across the fields, chatting about our schools, the subjects we were studying – they were all doing one or other of the sciences – and what we hoped for in the future. (We talked rather little about girls.) I loved, and still love, being in the country. The sweet calmness of it! (Of course I know it's cold and wild for much of the year, and gives the men who work it an arduous, chancy time.) Cheshire is a county of picturesque miniature scenery; little hills, little valleys, little roads winding in and out – I have already expatiated on them: hawthorn hedges and clumps of trees, cornfields and pastures. The sun would begin to sink, another evening to pass by . . .

I realise that a pastoral interlude of singular uneventfulness may give pleasure to its writer, but there isn't much in it for its reader. (Readers seem to be born with a craving for *events*.) From my spell of what greater writers than I would feel bound to call 'returning to one's roots', I can produce only one vividly memorable event. And, as must now be apparent, such events dredged up from my memory have a knack of turning out to be discreditable.

One summer evening we were drifting about in a field near my cousin's house. One of his friends had brought a gun with him, a gun he had for shooting pellets at wood-pigeons and rabbits. The other youths, who'd handled a gun before – I hadn't – took turns in trying it out, actually without a great deal of success, I thought.

'What about me?' I asked.

The gun was handed to me with some reluctance.

I held it according to the manner in which I'd seen the others holding it.

'What shall I aim at?' I asked.

'Nothing,' said my cousin.

'Why not?' I looked around. 'What about that cow?'

There was a cow standing sideways on, about fifty yards away; a big enough target for me to stand some chance of hitting it, and also big enough not to be harmed thereby.

I aimed.

'Harry!'

'Harry, you *can't*!'

'Oh, *can't I*?'

Wild success. The cow leapt in the air. I can still see it, its back legs up and its tail flying, exactly like an illustration of The Cow landing after it Jumped Over The Moon.

Someone seized the gun, with no resistance from me. After such a triumph I had no further plans for using it.

In the distance wood-pigeons went on burbling, the cuckoos calling.

I loved being in the country.

LXXIV

In those same days I was visiting, on my own, my mother's paternal relations as well. The mother and sister of my mother's father, J.K. (now disappeared). The sister, Sarah, was my mother's aunt, and I called her Great-Aunt Sally: her mother, known as Grandma Summerfield, was my great-grandmother. (Thus I can remember no less than three great-grandparents all alive at the same time in their nineties.)

Great-Aunt Sally's husband, who had taken over the ironmongery business when J.K. disappeared, was an active business-man whose high-minded Methodism consorted happily with making money. (It was said in the town that much of its most important business was conducted on the steps of Mill Street Wesleyan Chapel after service on Sunday mornings. For instance Mary Elizabeth, who frequented the Primitive Methodists, a social notch lower than the Wesleyans, kept a sharp eye on it – not, I suspect, that quite a lot of business wasn't conducted on the steps of the 'Prims'.) As a consequence of making a fair amount of money he had opened a second thriving shop in a different part of the town; and he had built a large house on the outskirts.

The house stood on rising ground some distance above the main road to Sandbach, approached by a curving drive between flowering bushes in a fair-sized garden. Behind the house was a very much larger garden, with two lawns separated by a ha-ha: the lower lawn was smoothed up to a crown to suit the playing of bowls; while on the upper lawn hoops could be driven into the ground for the playing of croquet. Beyond the lawns was a well-planted orchard sloping down finally to a brook. On one side of this estate there was a field which was hired out to a local farmer, on the other side an extensive kitchen garden where vegetables and fruit were grown. I can remember raspberry-canes under nets; gooseberry bushes from which I began to plunder hairy green fruits before they were ripe; currant bushes, redcurrant and blackcurrant; a bed of strawberries near the brook; and an asparagus-bed which, although it didn't seem to produce any edible heads early in the year, did sprout beautiful misty green fronds in the end. Also there was an enclosure for chickens – that meant fresh eggs. (We, my mother and father and sister and I, were beneficiaries of all these things.)

The house was typical of the 1920s, red brick in the lower half, grey stucco in the upper. There were outhouses that looked like stables, one of which was a garage for my great-uncle's motor-car, the other a laundry; there was a greenhouse where, in the summer, tomatoes were grown. Altogether pretty impressive to the likes of me. Out of doors there was a full-time gardener; indoors a cook-housekeeper and a daily housemaid – high on the wall in the kitchen was a small glass-fronted box in which hung a row of numbered indicator-plates of which, when a bell was rung elsewhere, one was set dangling furiously. And outside the kitchen window was a spindly spreading buddleia, whose long purple flowers were in summer simply covered with Red Admirals.

As well as being impressed I was in the early days slightly intimidated. My mother began taking me out to the house when I was quite small. I was particularly intimidated by Grandma Summerfield: she was tall, very upright and (in my eyes) very stately: she was never to be seen in anything but a well-fitting black dress that reached down to the ground. She walked with an elegant stick, and on top of her head she wore a widow's cap – a drooping circle of white lace with a black bow in the middle. Later on I concluded that she didn't personally mean to be intimidating: it was just her classic Victorian manner (which may well have been generally meant to be intimidating!). I learnt that she was really my step-great-grandmother. My great-grandfather's first wife died and he wanted to marry her sister. In England at that time it was illegal for a man to marry his deceased wife's sister. He discovered that on the other hand such a marriage was legal in Switzerland. So

137

to Switzerland they went. (Their Swiss marriage-certificate has finally come down to my hands – a strange document, evocative of determined love and peculiar laws.)

Great-Aunt Sally did not strike me as intimidating in manner, yet I was aware of a firm will in the background of her personality. She was thin and delicate-looking. The bones of her face looked fragile: her complexion was pale, her lips sensitive and purplish and somehow drawn flat rather than swelling into fulness. I thought she was overawed by her mother. She had no children. There was nothing uneasy about the atmosphere of her house, yet there was little of ease. When her mother died she seemed to cast off the state of being overawed, yet the atmosphere of the house did not really change.

I suppose I was about six when my mother took me regularly to tea on Thursday afternoons. (She must have taken me when I was younger to the family gathering which took place every Boxing Day.) First of all we sat in the sitting-room, where there was not much to amuse me. On the walls were two huge engravings; one was of soldiers embarking on a ship to go off to war, with jolly waving of their caps while wives and sweethearts shed a tear or two on the quay; the other was again of soldiers, what remained of them, disembarking, some bandaged, some on crutches, some carrying each other, while smiling wives held up babies and among them widows wept. (I took it that the war was the Crimean.) Both engravings were beautifully-truthful representations of human scenes; as I grew older I thought I should like ultimately to possess them; and I could have inherited them – if I'd ever had a place with enough room on the walls to hang them!

However, it is from the days when I was small that I can remember a really poignant occasion. After conversation in the sitting-room we went into the dining-room to have tea at the dining-table, my mother and I sitting on one side, Great-Aunt Sally on the other. Some of the quelling, if not the intimidating, nature of the occasion arose from tea being preceded by Grace. We bowed our heads over our plates. Great-Aunt Sally recited the Grace.

The poignant occasion? One afternoon Great-Aunt Sally looked at *me*, instead of reciting Grace, and said:

'Harry, will you please to say Grace for us?'

A speechless moment. I wriggled on my chair, stammered out –

'I don't know any Grace . . . '

I felt a sharp kick on my ankle. Naturally I turned to my mother.

'What are you kicking me for?'

The moment passed but I have never forgotten it. Needless to say I was taught what to recite as soon as my mother and I were walking down the drive to go home.

'For what we are about to receive, may the Lord make us thankful!' As simple as that. I can still recall it any day of the week seventy years later.

When I was eleven or so I was trusted to go occasionally on my own, and soon after that always on my own. I began to enjoy it. Sometimes before tea Great-Aunt Sally asked me to play the piano in the sitting-room. (The piano was stiff and out of tune.) Otherwise we went straight into the dining-room, where she talked to me interestedly and unpatronisingly about how I was getting on at school, what I thought of my chances in the examinations; and, later, why I wanted to go to a university and which one.

Sometimes before tea, when she was out of the room supervising the preparations, I would lean over the arm of my chair and lift out of a canterbury on the floor beside me copies of the *Manchester Guardian* and the *Methodist Recorder*. I didn't get on very well with the latter, but I was soon aware that the former was classier than the *Daily Chronicle*, which we took at home. (I had already diagnosed Mary Elizabeth's *Daily Sketch* as pretty low down on the scale.) And sometimes, if a longer time elapsed, I lifted one of the glass windows along the shelves of the bookcase beyond the canterbury and tried some of the books. Henry David Thoreau and Ralph Waldo Emerson – *Essays*!

However, the tea when it came was excellent. It was 'high tea' of a lady-like kind that was nevertheless substantial enough for a growing boy at teatime while not intended to stuff him out for the rest of the day. Sometimes a boiled egg; sometimes hot buttered tea-cakes with a china lid over the plate to keep them warm; and sometimes a jam I was never given anywhere else, marrow and ginger – succulent small chewy cubes of marrow in a clear golden ginger-flavoured syrup. Before it I recited Grace as if I'd practised it from the cradle.

When I was eating my tea my gaze might wander over the pictures on the walls. In the dining-room the pictures were family portraits. I recollect them chiefly as a Victorian array in heavy gilt frames. I studied them, wondering if there were any among the subjects to whom I had a physical resemblance myself. There was *one*. The hair on his pate was already thinning, while on his jaw it was burgeoning thickly, and yet . . . There was something about his rounded forehead, something about what I felt was a pointed chin under the beard, that convinced me . . . Who was that one? No prizes for guessing. The errant J.K., my grandfather.

I kept my conviction to myself. It only occurred to me later that it was strange to find *his* portrait on the wall of Great-Aunt Sally's house. It seemed to show a certain tolerance and perhaps forgiveness on the part of high-minded Methodists. Also perhaps an unspoken acknowledgement that his defection from Mary Elizabeth was not entirely without understandable human basis . . . I sat there, wondering about him.

After tea Great-Aunt Sally and I walked, if it were still light, in the garden, where she would cut me a bunch of flowers for my mother. When there were apples on the trees I was invited to pick some. I usually ate one on the spot – the crisp flesh, the sweet juice, the incomparable flavour of an apple just off the tree is quite unlike its flesh and its juice later on. When I bite into a Cox's Orange or a James Grieve or a Worcester Pearmain after it has been polished, packed and refrigerated for weeks, my memory reminds me in anguish of how utterly delicious it must once have tasted. In fact Great-Aunt Sally did store apples, Beauty of Bath, through the winter: they still smelt delightful but the skins tended to wrinkle, alas! (You have to remember that in those days weeks elapsed when there were practically no apples, other than brilliantly-red, woolly-fleshed Canadian ones in the shops.)

When finally I left to catch the bus I carried, as well as the bunch of flowers or foliage, a basket containing quantities of whatever fruit happened to be in season; perhaps tomatoes (also smelling quite different when just picked from the plant); and a dozen fresh eggs. Though the flowers and fruits were gifts, I had been given money to pay for the eggs. Aunt Sally would never have asked for it: it was my mother who had insisted – she would!

LXXV

Great-Aunt Sally used to ask me, as I got older, what books I was reading – so far as I recall, she was the only person who did. Consequently she began to occupy a special place in my imagination as 'someone I could talk to' about cultural things. I have already observed that she was interested in why I wanted to go to a university and which one. At first I had been vague in my reply about which one, but after having broken the news of my choice to my mother and father, the time came when I plucked up courage to tell Great-Aunt Sally. (Her choice of newspapers and books had stirred in me intimations of her 'cultural horizons' not being bounded by Crewe.) I said nervously:

'I thought of Cambridge.'

She showed neither shock nor disapproval – nor acceptance and approval, for that matter.

'That would be nice for you,' she said.

'It's *the* place for science,' I said.

'Yes.' (Had she known already? Probably not, yet possibly.)

I developed my case.

She asked me what my mother and father thought about it, and I told her they were thinking about it – giving the impression, I admit, that they were thinking about it with favour. I pointed out that it would depend on my winning a scholarship, of course.

'Yes,' she said, nodding her head thoughtfully. 'I hope you're successful.'

The conversation moved on to her usual intellectual stand-by – the books I was reading . . .

I recall that she recommended me warmly to read

Arnold Bennett – sprung from an equally good Wesleyan family, I thought, in the Potteries not thirty miles away.

I could not help wondering what she would think of the list of books I was accumulating, the main body of it assembled by courtesy of W. H. Smith & Son's circulating library to which my mother contributed a quarterly subscription. I was reading novels, and the list included works by such writers as Hall Caine (I remember *The Manxman*), Marie Corelli, Warwick Deeping and P. C. Wren (everybody was reading *Sorrell And Son* and *Beau Geste*), May Sinclair, Somerset Maugham (novels about Malaya), someone called Joan Sutherland (about whom I remember nothing but one title, *Sounding Brass*), Ethel M. Dell (unforgettable, *The Way Of An Eagle*), Elinor Glyn. (I can't swear that I ever read anything by Berta Ruck, whom I met, to my delight, in her old age: sprightly, tough and great fun – talking about piloting aeroplanes!) Best-sellers of the day. For one thing I feel they were not as bad as all that; and, compared with best-sellers of the present day, the impression they have left behind is of relative innocence and naturalness.

Anyone can see, though, that by letting the beastly Bodge put me off lessons in English literature from the age of fourteen I missed being supplied with a reading-list compiled by some supposedly knowledgeable person. (I bear in mind that I did spend the time usefully learning French.) I read what books I found for myself – uninstructed again! In the case of Smith's library my mother put me in the way of finding them, I suppose, yet I don't remember our discussing them. (My father, I think, didn't read much at all.) On the other hand I must concede that while under the tutelage of Bodge I read *David Copperfield* as a set-book and was so bowled over that I took *Oliver Twist* out of the negligibly small fiction library of CCSS, and asked for *Barnaby Rudge* as a birthday present. And also *Under The Greenwood Tree* as a set-book, with so much pleasure that I resolved to read *Tess Of The D'Urbervilles* later on.

Another boy in my class was a devotee of, not to say proselytiser for, Alexandre Dumas *père*. I kept up with him, reading novels by the series: *The Three Musketeers*, *The Count Of Monte Cristo* and other volumes incorporating shared characters. (I still own a copy of *Taking The Bastille* with a label in the cover indicating a School Prize – in the Fourth Form, when I must have been thirteen.) And of course when I came into the Science Sixth I took to the works of H. G. Wells, starting with the scientific romances and ending with the writings in which he trailed the idea of a World State – to bring wars between nations to an end – so rousing my imagination to a fervour which has never utterly vanished.

However, I have been saving up recall of my second main source of books, in order to amuse myself by scoring a point. Against W. H. Smith & Son as my first source, the second was the Mechanics' Institute. Whereas W. H. Smith & Son offered the town's housewives, with a bit of time on their hands and money to spare for a subscription, Hall Caine, Ethel M. Dell, Marie Corelli, Warwick Deeping; the Mechanics' Institute, originally set up for factory hands to train themselves in elementary engineering practice up to the point of enabling themselves to repair and maintain the machines of the Industrial Revolution, offered – for free! – novels by Jane Austen, Dickens, George Eliot, Hardy, Conrad. It was from the Mechanics' that I took out *Tess* and *Adam Bede* in honour of my paternal grandmother, Abigail; *The Card* (nobody having told me that *The Old Wives' Tale* was so much better) as a tribute to Great-Aunt Sally. Other novels by Dickens, other novels by Hardy. I'm sure I saw the title *War And Peace* among Foreign Literature, but for no reason whatsoever didn't catch on – and never read it for another ten years. I missed Anthony Trollope (now my favourite writer) altogether.

What now seems to me most remarkable among my peculiar random feats of schoolboy reading was my lighting upon, and taking to, the novels of Joseph Conrad. I read them enthusiastically. *Arrow of Gold*, *Lord Jim*, *Nostromo*. Totally unaware of metaphor and all that, I remember them well as a bit turgid, perhaps, but some of the best of rattling-good adventure stories!

LXXVI

The Crewe Branch of W. H. Smith & Son . . . I'm reminded – how could I forget?

The shop, situated in the market-less Market Square, was double-fronted with a funnel-shaped entrance, on one side of which was an open stall for newspapers and periodicals, at the end the door into the shop, where, right at the back, was the lending library. I was on my way to the library, on the pavement just beside one of the shop-windows. A wintry evening, tiny snowflakes falling, the shop-windows brightly illuminated, people passing me. I was thinking of my sister, then about five years old.

'Harry!'

I was stopped. It was the wife of one of the teachers at my father's school.

'I hear your sister's poorly.'

'Yes . . . '

'Very poorly?'

'The doctor just came this afternoon.'

'What did he say?'

'He thinks it's meningitis.'

'Oh.' She put her hand on my arm. 'I'm so sorry to hear that.'

I was unable to answer. I did not see her go away because tears were gushing from my eyes and beginning to roll down my cheeks. Uttering the name of the disease had suddenly faced me with its total reality – she might *die* of it. I wept.

In the event my sister recovered. Yet how could I ever forget that moment? For once I can see myself, standing alone on the dark pavement; but at the same time I see the books in the illuminated shop-window as I saw them, the colours of their jackets suddenly heightened, the sharpness of their edges suddenly dissolved . . .

LXXVII

Thoughts of Great-Aunt Sally's garden and its fruits remind me of the joys of seasonality that have disappeared with the constant importing into our country of fruits and vegetables from lands far away (usually reprehensible lands such as South Africa, Chile, Turkey, Israel), where the seasons are different and the fruits and vegetables grown there look just as fresh after being frozen and artificially ripened, even if they taste different.

I can still remember the day in a year when garden peas first came into the shops: Mary Elizabeth served them on their own, for each of us a saucer holding a little heap of them, lightly dusted with pepper, a nut of butter in the middle. We *savoured* them. The same with new potatoes: we always ate the first of them on their own, lightly boiled with a sprig of mint, and again a nut of butter on top. And tomatoes – I can't remember when I last held to my nose a tomato that gave off that utterly identifiable fresh-from-the-leaves fragrance of the tomatoes from Great-Aunt Sally's greenhouse, a very faintly acrid fragrance in the same vein as that of celery.

On the other hand I have to admit that we were not entirely deprived of exotic fruits from abroad. Every few weeks I would go with Mary Elizabeth to Manchester, to a warehouse where she stocked up, at a discount, with goods for her front-shop – chiefly clothing, bed-linen, soap, etc. On the way back from the warehouse on the road leading up to London Road Station (now rechristened something else), there was an expensive greengrocer's/fruiterer's shop, Dingley's it was called. And from Dingley's Mary Elizabeth would sometimes buy a pineapple, sometimes peaches, sometimes nectarines. Bliss it was to be eating those fruits a couple of hours later! I shall never forget the delighted surprise with which I tasted the difference in flavour, from that of a peach, of my first nectarine.

LXXVIII

And now I come to the point where I must declare my debt of gratitude to Auntie Mag. These were the days when she was extending my 'cultural horizons' beyond the boundaries of Crewe.

Her home was in a little side-street – it was not far from my painter-cum-decorator grandfather's. Unlike her parents and brother, with whom she lived, she had what I mean to call, with admiration rather than snobbery, cultural aspirations. (Her brother's only interest in life was keeping racing-pigeons: they were housed in a wire-netted aviary at the end of the little backyard, and I remember the wicker baskets in which they were transported to distant places whence to fly home.) Auntie Mag's cultural aspirations were apparent in her speech. Her voice was contralto, soft and nicely-modulated, and her pronunciation was carefully lifted above the dialect of the town. Broad vowels were narrowed in a stylised way; consonants meticulously sounded, especially the initial aspirate. Where racey usage led most people to say 'Has 'e gone?', Auntie Mag would always say 'Has he gone?' Stylised and meticulous, her speech nevertheless fell agreeably on the ear, though, by now self-conscious about my own speech, it did not occur to me there and then to copy hers.

Auntie Mag was tall and willowy, unmarried; she had a schoolmistress friend, also unmarried, who was short and stocky. On Saturdays the two of them – the tall and the small – made cultural excursions to Chester, Manchester, Liverpool, Hanley. (I imagined it was in this spirit that Auntie Mag and my mother, when they were friends in their pupil-teacher days, had made joint expeditions, one of which, frequently recalled by my mother, had been a trip down the Rhine a few years after the turn of the century.)

I was twelve or thirteen when Auntie Mag first invited me to accompany her friend and herself on one of their excursions. Thereafter she invited me more frequently, and when I was fifteen or so regularly. To think of myself, a boy of fifteen, sixteen, seventeen, walking round Chester, going to the theatre in Liverpool, to concerts in Hanley, with two mature maiden ladies now seems pretty odd; then it didn't seem odd at all. And also, having been introduced into this kind of thing by Auntie Mag, I began a bit later to make similar excursions to these places by myself. (On Saturday afternoons spent at home I went to shout in football matches on the school playing-field.)

To Chester we went mainly for its historical charms. We walked on top of the wall built by the Romans to defend the town from attack along the river boundary; from this vantage point we caught views of the River Dee, and beyond it the racecourse called the Roodee. (In the river there was salmon: Mary Elizabeth always gave us Dee salmon for dinner on Good Friday.) The red sandstone cathedral of Chester remains in my memory as rather squat and heavy: we occasionally ventured in and I remember hearing Evensong there (though it would not surprise me now to hear that there was no Evensong on a Saturday afternoon). Then the two ladies liked to wander round the superior shops which were built unusually in two tiers on either side of a main street: one climbed a staircase from the first tier to reach a balcony along which the second tier had their fronts. For years I thought this architectural curiosity was enigmatically called The Rose, till I saw the name printed later – The Rows.

To Hanley we went for concerts, sometimes in mid-week. Celebrity Concerts in which artists of international reputation performed. The one who stands out in my recollections was called Vladimir Pachman, a little ancient Jewish man who took ages to adjust the height of his piano-stool: it would not have surprised me if he ended up by demanding a sheet of paper to slip under one of the legs – in fact I'm not sure on second thoughts that he actually didn't slide a sheet under one of the legs of the piano. In the course of his performance he talked to the audience between the pieces, and sometimes during the pieces. His touch, I feel I have never since heard the like of, was always described as light as a butterfly: I remember his playing a Chopin Study so lightly that one almost wondered if one had actually heard it.

To Liverpool and Manchester we went for theatres and art galleries. In Manchester we went to see what would nowadays be called popular pieces, plays imported from the West End of London, musical comedies (later called 'musicals'). It was to see the musicals that I went by myself. Cochran Revues I recall as by the standards of those days highly sophisticated (and possibly by the standards of these days highly sophisticated). And the first of the American musicals to be imported – I recalled *Good News* as unprecedentedly vigorous and brassy and having an effect on the audience which I then couldn't give a name to – and for which I might now consider the word 'sexy'. What I don't recall, because I missed it, to a regret that has lasted a lifetime, was Diaghileff's Ballets Russes. (I could make up for missing *War And Peace* by reading it ten years later: I could never make up for missing the Russian Ballet.)

In Liverpool we went to the Playhouse, a repertory theatre that was just launched on its way to fame. I saw plays by Shaw, Chekhov and suchlike, marvellous plays. The quality of the plays was so marvellous that, although many of the actors and actresses and producers subsequently became national figures, from then on it was the quality of a play which became my prime interest in the theatre, way ahead of any interest in the acting and production. (I haven't changed.)

However, the star of my reminiscences was a girl I saw in a Commedia dell' Arte piece. Columbine, playing opposite a tall, athletic Harlequin, she was small and funny-looking, quicksilver-like, enchanting. If I'd had the courage I should have waited outside the stage-door. Another dream found its way into my thoughts, a dream of someone I should never meet but only see in the distance on the stage . . . Then by an amazing coincidence, a couple of years later in casual conversation with a fellow undergraduate who came from the region, her name came up. He *knew* her! So in the next vacation we went to the theatre and in her dressing-room I met her. As quicksilver-like as she was on the stage, and as funny-looking. I was entranced. If only! I could see no way whatsoever of following up the introduction: our lives and everything about our ways of life, let alone the geography of it all, were too far apart.

But the image of her shone in my imagination – and served me for the heroine of the first novel I was to write, *Trina*, published under my real name in 1934 by Heinemann (and nowadays occasionally advertised by sellers of secondhand books at an extraordinary price).

LXXIX

During these years my father was encouraging me to play golf. He belonged to a club a few miles out of the town and we went there on our bicycles. It was a pretty nine-hole course; and golf, I could see, was an attractive game.

But . . . Here I have to refer to my taking it into my head, when I was aged eight or nine, that all the other boys in the school playground were bigger and stronger than me. My father's efforts to encourage me to play golf had the effect of making me feel I was born to be an aesthete rather than athlete. Where I'd got hold of that dichotomy I can't remember, and it now seems to me so ridiculous that I find it difficult to write about it equably – ridiculous as a general idea, and even more ridiculous in being applied to me personally.

My father was an athletic man: at Westminster College he had excelled in sports. He had the physique for it. He was shortish, firmly-built in a not-too-heavy way. He was quite good-looking, with large grey eyes in deep orbits, a slightly beaky nose, and thick straight hair of which he had scarcely lost any by the time he died. (Here I would like to record that my mother, too, was good-looking. Her eyes were greyish-blue, her nose straight if perhaps a shade too long, and her hair auburn – or 'sandy' or 'carrotty' in unkind parlance – and wavy. Wedding-photographs show them as a very nice-looking pair.)

My trouble was that, when my father and I were playing golf, I felt that I could never beat him. Don't ask my why I ever thought I should! I was a beginner and he was one of the best players in the club: I still possess a set of silver spoons which he accumulated from winning regular club competitions. (Actually they are silver-plated.) And it's absolutely essential for me to say that he was never anything but encouraging and sensible – after all, he was a teacher by profession and by instinct. Never did he say anything or do anything to affect me with the feeling that I could never be as good at the game as he. Not that I didn't enjoy the game. I remember lovely summer mornings – we played before the course became crowded – when there was dew on the grass (especially in the rough), and a faint mist round the trees; not to mention the mornings when I started off with a drive straight down the fairway.

An aesthete rather than an athlete. It was not until

I took up squash in my twenties that I discovered I was strong enough, and had a good enough eye for the ball, to give some of my contemporaries, bigger and stronger than me, a good game, even beat them. And furthermore I discovered a liking, like my father's, for hearty athletic company.

If only!

When one remarks of somebody that he has taken an idea into his head, what one ought to do first of all is to examine his head rather than the idea.

LXXX

My father had a liking for athletic company: he used to play golf every Saturday and on light evenings during the week, excepting Sundays. He was innately sociable: he enjoyed most forms of company – yet he did not indulge his taste greatly. He sometimes stayed at the golf club after his game, stayed, but not for long, occasionally for a bottle of beer. My mother instantly noticed the brightness in his eye when he got home – not with overt disapproval, but not with an emotion that could be mistaken for encouragement. We were not a teetotal household, but there was rarely much alcohol in the house – small amounts of brandy for medicinal purposes; of whisky for my father's preference in the white sauce on Christmas pudding; and of port for consumption with a raw egg as a pick-me-up. I myself never tasted beer until I was an undergraduate. (On the other hand there was an unforgettable occasion when, because I was thought to be in a debilitated state of health, I had nipped home during playtime for a raw egg and port; and when I got back to school was directly regimented into a lecture – the smell of port on my breath – on 'The Evils Of Drink'.)

The other occasions when my father came home with a certain brightness in his eye were when he had been to his Masonic Lodge. He was a Freemason, much to the malicious amusement of my mother and myself. We made fun of the boyish secret society; of the myths we had picked up about their rituals, such as being taught funny handshakes and being made to take down their trousers for the initiation ceremony. He had a little Masonic apron made of white kid, very pretty – I think it was decorated with pale-blue ribbon somewhere. And a little 'bible' composed of hieroglyphics which were supposed to defeat the curiosity of anyone who was not in the secret. (In middle age I inherited from my mother's family a book, handwritten and bound in white kid, where the rigmarole was exposed *en clair* – not very impressive, I thought.)

However, I think there was a deeper element in our unkind fun. We had taken the point, admirable enough, that the Brotherhood gave money to charity; also the point that its members 'helped each other on' in the world. To my mother's eye, and in my father's half-admission, there was plenty of the latter going on in the town. To this day I regard Town Councils with suspicion, and anybody in the property-business and the building-trade as liable to be crooked. Not that my father had the slightest connection with the property-business or the building-trade; and as a schoolteacher he seemed to be very little 'helped on' by the Brotherhood. Among his peers he was about the last to get a headmastership.

So my mother contrived to rail against the Freemasons simultaneously on two opposite counts: that the Brotherhood did things they ought not to be doing; and that the said Brotherhood had done nothing for *him*. In fact as I see it now, my father, a nice man, was innately under-endowed with that gift, which I have come to observe as universally necessary, the gift for pushing oneself to the front. (Is it any surprise that I, for my part, say, 'Sod those genes!')

In due course, though, my father did become Worshipful Master, or whatever it was called, of his Lodge. My belief is that he was a Freemason because he was sociable and enjoyed the company of his fellow human beings. (At home we rarely had any company other than that of Auntie Mag two or three nights a week for bridge.) When he became Worshipful Master my mother wanted to evade being at his side at official do's. (I don't think she ever set foot in the golf club.) Alas, perhaps because of what she had suffered in her early life, perhaps because of what was innate, she was inhibited from the giving of oneself to company, from that trusting of oneself, if only just a little way, to one's fellow human beings, which underlies the act of being sociable. She did go with him to the celebration of being 'installed', and I remember how pleasingly got-up for the occasion she looked. And yet . . .

The other activity of my father's which I remember was his being local secretary for the National Union of Teachers. Being local secretary of the NUT entailed quite a lot of clerical work, and I used to help him sometimes by copying letters and addressing envelopes. A few months ago, now, when I was walking down a London street to somewhere else, I happened to look up and notice – for the first time in my life – the sign, Mabledon Place. Instantly I saw the address I had copied on to scores of letters: Hamilton House, Mabledon Place . . . The address of the NUT headquarters. In view of the way schoolteachers have been treated in the 1980s, I felt proud of my father's work in the 1920s.

155

My mother, although she approved of these activities in principle, deplored the amount of time he spent on them without being paid; but really she was seriously moved, I think, by a feeling that they lessened his chances of promotion to a headmastership. She may have been right. The town's affairs were ruled by Tories. (She and my father voted Liberal.) Even as a schoolboy, not 'politically aware', I somehow could not understand how Crewe, an unrelievedly working-class town, came to return for years as its Member of Parliament – I can even remember his name, Sir Joseph Davies – a Conservative!

LXXXI

It seems to me as incredible as it's shameful that the only thing I can remember about the General Strike – I was fifteen – is reading in the newspapers that Oxford and Cambridge undergraduates were driving locomotives, steam locomotives.

LXXXII

Now the prospect of examinations in which my performance was vital for what I wanted to do. To go up to Cambridge. Just that, and nothing else. Cambridge – the place for scientists . . . My performance was vital because on examinations I had to win a scholarship. My parents could not afford to send me to Cambridge without my winning a scholarship. The prospect was dominated by *money*.

My plan was to take Higher School Certificate in June, then the Cambridge Entrance Scholarships in the following December: then Higher School Certificate for the second time in the following June. The fact that my birthday was in August meant that I was always taking examinations at what seemed an early age. I was sixteen when I took Higher School Certificate for the first time, and seventeen, obviously, when I took it for the second.

I pored over the Universities Handbook and chose a College to aim at. None of my teachers had been to Oxford or Cambridge, so there was nobody inside the school to advise me, less than nobody outside. In the past I had differentiated between the Colleges only on the basis of their beautiful coats-of-arms illustrated in my collection of cigarette-cards. With more information now to hand I settled for the College which had numbered Milton and Darwin among its members. Under Bodge I had borne with *Comus* and *Lycidas* for School Certificate; but the Theory of Evolution, which I hadn't studied at all, must – because even I knew it explained how we come to be here without the invention of any supernatural agency – be right up my street.

The first obstacle: I discovered that both Oxford and Cambridge demanded a certain – it turned out to be pretty small – proficiency in Latin or Greek. When offered the alternative of Latin or German as a second language after French for School Certificate, I had of course chosen German. For something that Cambridge University called Previous Examination, I had to learn enough Latin in a matter of months. My parents were prepared to fork out for some private coaching, so I consulted the school's Latin master. He was an amiable man, a big rolling-voiced fellow – and incidentally one of the staff's small covey of gents. He

157

agreed. So every Saturday morning for a couple of terms I rode my bicycle out to his house for a lesson.

I can't say that I fell in love with learning Latin, as I had fallen in love with learning French and German; but mastering just a little left me a residue of impatience with people who didn't know a word of it, with English people who even had no intimations of which words in their own language, let alone which rules of its grammar, derived from Latin. (The first notice one reads on sailing up the Thames estuary from the Continent – *Port of London Authority*. Leaving out the 'of', Latin from beginning to end!) The set-books were an Ode by Horace; a passage from *De Bello Gallico*, more concerned with logistics than fighting; and Cicero's speech, *Pro Milone*, which I readily took to be a matter of one crooked individual defending another crooked individual – a phenomenon I've since come to realise hasn't changed in over a thousand years. I learnt by heart the translation of key-passages in *Pro Milone*, so that when the examination paper required me to translate a slab from the text, it was only a question of identifying the opening words and closing words for me to be well away. I passed the examination.

To take the examination I had to go for the first time to Cambridge, and to stay for a night in the College of my choice. I can still see the First Court as I saw it for the first time, when coming in from the busy street by the tunnel-like gateway below the tower – the low greyish Tudor buildings along its sides, a verdant circular lawn in the middle, the Chapel in one corner and the loftier Dining Hall beside it, wistaria growing up the walls. I had never been anywhere like it before, with its backwaterish quiet, its domestic scale, its unassertive penetrating beauty . . . I knew I must, must, must come here. I slept the night on a broken-down hospital bed in an undergraduate's room with no heating and just one item of indoor sanitation – under the said broken-down hospital bed. (For more serious matters of evacuation one had to walk round the Court to a separate establishment behind some bushes.) I must, must, must come here . . . Milton and Darwin.

The second obstacle I have already explained. I had to win a scholarship. There were two alternatives: one was to win a College Scholarship in an open examination set by the Colleges; the other to win a scholarship by performance in the Higher School Certificate examination. I wrote in for specimens of the College examination papers – and suffered an unforgettable shock. The questions were set for a level of knowledge miles above that required for HSC questions. I could scarcely attempt them, and saw no likelihood of being able to do more on the strength of what I was currently being taught for HSC. The only answer was private coaching out of school. I approached each of my science teachers in turn.

Each of them refused.

I was desolate. I thought they were ill-willed and lazy. For years they had been teaching nothing beyond the HSC syllabus – nobody had ever asked them to go beyond it. To coach me for the Cambridge examinations they might have to do a bit of swotting up themselves: they couldn't be bothered to do it, even for money. (I have to say that it never occurred to me at the time that in their eyes I might be an uppity boy making a fearful nuisance of himself.) However, I found an ally, another boy in the Form – we became the first two boys at CCSS who wanted to go to Cambridge. (I should like to say that *he* was definitely not an uppity boy making a fearful nuisance of himself – he is the boy whom I have previously described unkindly as religious in a giggly way and wanting to become an Anglo-Catholic clergyman.

We became friendly in alliance. I will call him T.M.)

So that was that. I think it was at this stage that my parents paid for me to have a correspondence course in Physics, but I could see that it was not going to be much help. It was one thing to mug up enough Latin from scratch to get through 'Little Go'; but quite another to mug up enough Physics, Chemistry and Mathematics from HSC level to get a College Scholarship. The prospect was hopeless; but I took the scholarship examination all the same, in order to spend a few more nights – possibly my last – in the College.

In the meantime I had had my first shot at Higher School Certificate. The result was creditable enough for me to pick up, somewhere along the line, a residential scholarship to Manchester University; and to Liverpool University a lesser award going by the name of Morgan – I remember referring to it, in memory of Auntie Nell's runabout, as my Three-Wheeler Scholarship.

But everything hung on the result of my second shot at Higher School Certificate. Two kinds of scholarship: one awarded by the County, which would not give me enough to go to Cambridge; the other awarded by the State, which could. For a State Scholarship one had to get Distinctions in all three subjects. Everything hung on that; and that depended on work, on swot . . .

LXXXIII

Although I increased the number of hours during which I sat solitarily at my desk in the boxroom, I wasn't going to be temporarily defeated in my pursuit of 'culture'. I persisted in going to the theatre with or without Auntie

Mag, in Liverpool and Manchester. I did my piano practice as much as ever – still lingering in my teacher's music-room at the end of my lesson, or in the street outside an hour later, in order to exchange a few more sentences, despite recognising that the hope of their leading to anything of greater import was non-existent, face to beautiful face in the dusk with K.H. The concession I made to swotting was to go less frequently to the cinema.

It happened that T.M. was devoted to the cinema. Our common aspiration towards Cambridge drew us together, though he was not the sort of boy I was drawn to in the ordinary way. He was tall and thin and mildly fragile: he had once suffered from a mastoid abscess and he constantly wore a wad of cotton-wool in his ear – I thought it was sometimes smelly. However, he was lively and entertaining company. He too was trying to find 'culture' in Crewe, and for his part it consisted of going to the pictures three or four times a week. At one time I used to go with him. The films were in black and white, and the showing was accompanied by music played on a broken-down piano. The pianist was situated down below the left-hand corner of the screen, whence, it seemed to me, it must be extraordinarily difficult for him to see what it was he was supposed to be accompanying: I had nothing but admiration for his efforts.

Thanks to T.M. I saw some of the Masterpieces of the Silent Screen. I remember *Intolerance* (still shown to highbrow film-clubs), where an actress called Lillian Gish (still alive and acting) floated down-river in a snowstorm on what I now remember as an ice-floe, though that can't be correct. We giggled throughout posturing performances by Mary Pickford, whose golden ringlets were to be associated with sunshine. (We had to take that, in black and white, on trust.) Charlie Chaplin in a log-cabin on the edge of a cliff, incredibly funny. Clark Gable as the pilot of an aeroplane, not at all funny. And, the opposite of a source for giggling, the most beautiful and moving face I had ever, and still have ever, seen on the screen or anywhere else, the face of Greta Garbo . . . (Actually, forty years later, I did see that face in the flesh, half-hidden under a wide felt hat, only a few feet away from me: she was entirely alone on a January evening in New York, climbing in her fur coat round a huge pile of dirty snow heaped on the deserted sidewalk of Park Avenue. Momentarily we looked at each other. Oh, that *face*, that *soul*!)

While thinking about cinema-going in Crewe, I'm dismayed to realise that I've been singularly ungracious about Crewe's own 'cultural offerings' – and, come to that, CCSS's too. Crewe had a small theatre I recall as pleasing inside; when one sat down in one's seat one was confronted with an oil-cloth safety-curtain covered in a mosaic of advertisements for local businesses and shops. The theatre was visited by touring companies of repute, Sir Frank Benson's in Shakespeare, the Carl Rosa in opera. It was here that I heard Sir John Martin Harvey recite, in more than all seriousness if that is possible, 'It is a far far better thing', etc. And it was here that I saw the Carl Rosa's *Carmen*, the Carl Rosa's *La Bohème* – I was bowled over.

The offerings of CCSS were Gilbert and Sullivan operettas performed by the Old Boys' and Old Girls' Society. I went to the performances with great enthusiasm every night, learnt many of the lyrics, especially of *The Mikado*. My big, rolling-voiced Latin teacher played Pooh Bah, my lively little Chemistry master (also a gent) played Ko-Ko. I should have loved to take part; but even had I become an Old Boy – what a thought! – it seems unlikely that I should ever have been selected for even a lowly part in the chorus, as the performances were rehearsed and conducted by Bodge!

In the last two terms before my crucial second shot at Higher School Certificate I cut down my cinema-going with T.M. to one night per week. No companies of repute came to the New Theatre in Crewe. The Old Boys and Girls had in the previous term shot their bolt for the year. Auntie Mag tactfully invited me to no more than a couple of plays of the highest cultural order at the Liverpool Playhouse. Work, work, work; swot, swot, swot . . . Cooped up in the boxroom. Having hot drinks or cold drinks, according to the day's being cold or hot, brought up to me by my mother.

LXXXIV

Suddenly I recall an incident, a ridiculous incident from this time. It was the era, short-lived, when the undergraduates of Oxford University took to a fashion for wearing trousers that were exceptionally wide, thence known as 'Oxford bags'. I decided I must have some, but at the time I didn't know that undergraduates wore them with blazers or sports jackets. So I went to Bobby Moseley and had a whole suit made for me. A beautiful light tweed, in a herring-bone pattern of pale grey and blue. I put on the suit for the first time when I was going to my music-lesson (for obvious reasons). I remember that it was a warm summer evening, with late sunshine illuminating the grey and blue of the tweed. Near to my music-teacher's house I happened to catch sight of myself passing a shop-window. In the pale colours, with yards of material flapping round my legs, I looked as if I had come out in my pyjamas.

LXXXV

Ten days before the examination my sister went down with mumps. She was isolated in her room – I forget all the rigmarole of precaution, which was in any case otiose. Three days before the examination *I* went down with mumps.

Crisis in the home. The doctor was called in. The school was communicated with.

I simply had to take the examination.

What saved the day was that although my sister had two mumps, one on each side of her jaw, I had one mump only, on the left. Bearing in mind that mumps can be more serious for a male than for a female, our doctor decided nevertheless that I might risk it. I had a sizeable lump on the neck: I was commanded to report instantly any symptoms in the groin.

A little room was set aside for me in a wing of the school. A desk and a chair. The door was locked, and with my head and neck wrapped in a scarf I climbed through the window. At the appropriate hour a master came along outside and handed me my question-paper through the window. I sat down at the desk and wrote.

When it was time to stop writing a master came to the window and told me to climb out, leaving the examination answers behind on the desk. Then the room and the examination papers were fumigated by a caretaker opening the door just wide enough to push into the room a fire-shovel on which a piece of sulphur had been set alight. Naturally I never saw him do it, but the sulphurous fumes constantly hanging in the air proved that he had – and didn't make my head feel any clearer next morning. The routine was followed day after day. By the time the examination was over my sister's mumps had disappeared. And for me the risk had been justified. Not only did the lump on my neck subside, but one in my groin never came up – so Posterity was safe.

And the result of the examination? Distinctions in all three subjects.

LXXXVI

The result of the examination, Distinctions in all three subjects – but what was this? *No* indication beside the published result that I had qualified for a State Scholarship.

No State Scholarship. I couldn't go to Cambridge.

At home we couldn't believe it. My father went to the Headmaster of the school, and *he* said he couldn't believe it. He contracted to write to the Examining Board.

It was no State Scholarship for me. And the explanation? My marks were almost equal in all three subjects: the essential necessity for a State was to score a particularly high mark in just one subject. We gathered that with a few more marks in just one subject, at the expense of a few less divided between the two, I could have got by. Hard luck!

Hard luck. That was that.

LXXXVII

I simply couldn't bear to give up. Nor could my mother and father. Money. (I was accepted for a place in the College.) My mother and father, unbeknownst to me, had taken the only remaining step they could think of.

I had never believed – nor could imagine myself ever believing – in a *deus ex machina*. In this case my beliefs were confounded, by the materialisation of a *dea*. Great-Aunt Sally.

Great-Aunt Sally was prepared to make me an interest-free loan of £1000 for an indefinite period. (I learnt later that if it had not been paid by Great-Aunt Sally's death, it was to come out of money she was bequeathing to my mother as a fair inheritance in restitution of family money which might have come to her from Great-Aunt Sally's brother, my mother's father, the errant J.K.

I was saved.

LXXXVIII

An interpolation at the last minute – and not in line with my previous free-wheeling recollections at that. Provoked by coming across a document – I said I had no documents. I remembered it only when I saw it, long after it was written. It ties up a loose end in what has gone before, when I recalled my mother's fears that I might be starting off at CCSS on the wrong foot as a consequence of her early quarrel with the Headmaster – fears which I merely said, leaving a loose end, turned out to be justified. The document was the personal reference provided by the Headmaster for the purpose of supporting my application for entry to a university – Cambridge!

By the time it turned up my career had included years in the Civil Service Commission, where I had read personal references galore, ranging from the unrestrainedly laudatory to the frankly warning-off; with somewhere in between the type I cared for least, calculatedly ambiguous – explicitly supporting, implicitly not worth the paper it was written on . . . My reference from CCSS, on a measly half-sized slip of headed school paper, was written in my own hand, signed by the Headmaster—

H. S. Hoff is a man of utmost probity and honour. I recommend him.

An innocent youth at the time, I had taken it at face value. Now, with the slip of paper in my hand again, I saw it differently—

'The dirty dog!' I cried.

He had even made me write the thing, at his dictation, in my own hand. Insult to injury.

In fury I tore it up. My mother's feeling that the old enmity lived on had turned out to be right.

In due course I calmed down. It occurred to me that it wasn't necessary to invoke a lifelong enmity towards my mother as explanation. When one came to think of it, my persistent out-of-step behaviour as a pupil at the school could scarcely have endeared me to any headmaster, whether he hated my mother or not. It *must* have been noticed, I realised now, that I regularly did a bunk from lessons that didn't interest me, that I made no attempt to conceal a low opinion of some of the masters; and to crown all, instead of going quietly along with the rest to Manchester or Liverpool University, I had insisted on aiming at Cambridge. A wilful, haughty, tiresome boy.

Otherwise described as a man of utmost probity and honour.

Who could be furious when confronted with that juxtaposition? I began to laugh.

I was in a position now to go on laughing. Whether or not the reference was intended to dish my chances –

167

I supposed my interpretation was open to some doubt – it had not succeeded.

My application to Cambridge had been accepted: two months after it was written, I was on my way there!

LXXXIX

A winter's dusk, the College gateway alive with people and voices.

A Tudor cavern with a huge oak gate at present folded back against the wall, in the middle of that gate a narrow door just wide enough to admit one person – like a cat-flap in a house door. (After 10 p.m. only the narrow door would be open, guarded by the College porter, ready to take down the name of any undergraduate committing the crime of coming in 'late'.) Most of the illumination of the cavern came from the window of the porter's lodge, opposite the folded-back gate, where the porter, a little man with both hair and face the same washed-out colour as if they had never been exposed to daylight, sat with his bowler-hat on indoors. It was nearly time for members of the College to dine together in Hall.

It was my first evening. The people crowding around me were my fellow undergraduates, all of them men, of course. (Women were not to be admitted to the College for another fifty years.) All around me public-school accents, borne on voices bold, confident and loud. (Were they so bold, confident and loud as to seem, in retrospect, a shade vulgar?) At the time I felt overwhelmed. Perhaps I ought to remark that boys from grammar schools, let alone secondary schools, were as rare among Cambridge undergraduates as robins among starlings. I felt like a robin among starlings, anyway.

I had cycled in from my digs on the other side of the river, comfortable digs with a bathroom next door to the bedroom and a piano in the sitting-room. (It was only in one's third year, I had been given to understand, that one had rooms in College.) The other man sharing my digs, although he was no more than six months older than me, seemed at least a couple of years older – I had just turned eighteen. He was a clergyman's son who had been to Repton, and he was clearly a nice man. Yet I felt slightly frightened of him.

I had dumped my bicycle, as my fellow undergraduates appeared to be dumping theirs, against the outside wall of the College; and then I came to find myself in the echoing cavern, echoing and old, dark and noisy. I looked at my fellow undergraduates. I'd got to Cambridge! The echoing voices, bold and confident with their public-school accents, made me realise that for the first time in my life I was surrounded by the upper-classes *en masse*.

They all looked bigger and stronger than me!